# The MOJO of Multidimensional Manifesting

*Unlocking True Abundance*
*Through Spiritual Ascension*

## Cynthia Clark

**Cynthia Clark LLC, Ascension17.com**

Cynthia Clark LLC books may be ordered through booksellers or by contacting:

Cynthia Clark LLC
P.O. Box 1304
Sedona, AZ 86339-1304
www.Ascension17.com
1-877-327-6095


ISBN: 979-8-9894495-0-7 (e)
ISBN: 979-8-9894495-1-4 (sc)
ISBN: 979-8-9894495-2-1 (a)

# CONTENTS

MANIFESTER

This book is dedicated to all those from the unseen realm who have been assisting me throughout my life, including my Higher Self, ancestors, spiritual guides, angels, Archangels, Ascended Masters, the Pleiadian Council of Light, the Arcturians, Andromedans, Sirians and Hathors. Thank you for guiding me in my spiritual path.

# ACKNOWLEDGEMENTS

This book could not have been possible without the assistance of several beautiful spiritual beings. First, I would like to thank my husband, Pat, for your ongoing support and encouragement. As my biggest fan, you keep me grounded and anchored when I have doubts, I love you very much. I would also like to thank my editor, Karen Connington. Your insights and attention to detail have made this work polished and presentable in a way I couldn't have done on my own. I'd also like to thank all of you have read various drafts of my book or assisted in some way, including Sheila Tye, Rob McClintic, Dr. Davia Coutcher, Lisha R. Joiner, Elizabeth Mead, Jim fellow Pleiadian and Ghandolff the Grateful. I appreciate your feedback and encouragement to keep going. Finally, I'd like to thank all my clients who have kept me anchored in my own path of ascension. It has been a pleasure working and interacting with you throughout the past two decades.

# FOREWORD

Cynthia is tapped into the world of spirit. There is no doubt her heart is channeling the information she shares throughout this book. If you are looking to be inspired, to feel hope that there is more to you and the world around you, more than what you experience with your five senses, then this book is for you. As we move from the age of proof to the age of belief, we need to have the tools and guidance to connect to our inner knowing with confidence. To truly "know" there is more to our being than what we have been taught. Cynthia so brilliantly shares methods for navigating an accelerating world. The MOJO of Multidimensional Manifesting is a book on living in a spirit-based reality. It provides a reassuring, step-by-step pathway to reconnecting to our inner truth.

We live in a quantum reality, yet only experience about 10% of our potential. When we begin to co-create with spirit, we open up to the other 90% so many will never tap into. Each of us has Divine superpowers that communicate with the world around us. The MOJO of Multidimensional

Manifesting guides us into knowing what the quantum world is saying so that we can begin living our best life. It begins to shape our reality in higher frequencies. This book shows us how to feel our personal power, to listen to this power, and move outside the looping cycle of doubt, fear and uncertainty. Our innate being is always there to be experienced. In this brilliant book you will learn to manage your own energy so you can put your heart's desire in the forefront and live your destiny: A life that is authentically YOU.

The MOJO of Multidimensional Manifesting covers all the bases, from intuition to a step-by-step guide to manifesting. The principles and methods are unraveled through Cynthia's heart-felt personal journey. The book is an activation of frequency. It holds you in a field so that you can know beyond the mind that you truly are Divine!

Because the frequency around you and within you is accelerating, many of us have become more sensitive or empathic. Emotions can shift your life as you are affected by the subtle energies. This book teaches you how to navigate the world of energy, a world as FREQUENCY.

My passion is to awaken the Quantum Body and Become 100% human potential—to experience the other 90% of our DNA, mind and body as Quantum. When I started Becoming BioQuantum DMT Academy in 2020, I was shocked by how many people did not trust in their inner guidance or were not even sure what that meant. After over 30 years on this journey, I have found learning the basic foundation of communicating with the world through energy, is the NEXT in human evolution. If you are ready to discover your next, to experience your MOJO as the powerful being you truly are, then this book is what you are looking for! Cynthia will guide you into your NEXT, a Life BeYOND what you can imagine. Cynthia is a Master!

Jewels Arnes, Founder of Becoming BioQuantum
BecomingBioQuantum.com

# PROLOGUE

If you have picked up this book, I'm guessing you are a spiritual individual and you are interested in doing more with your life. I'm also assuming that you are open to channeled guidance and the nuances of the universe beyond what you can see with your eyes. I believe that the universe is filled with magic, abundance and miracles if we only know how to fully open ourselves to it. I also believe that we are much more than just a human body, having one individual life. We are going to explore what it means to be multidimensional.

One aspect of multidimensionality includes some robust topics including reincarnation — that is living many, perhaps thousands of lifetimes in order to fine-tune our soul's objectives. A recent Pew Research study noted that reincarnation "is a view held by a substantial minority of the population," 33 percent to be exact. Thirty eight percent of American adults under 50 share the belief with the same number of American Catholics, and nearly half of Hispanic Catholics—amazing statistics among groups whose religious doctrine stringently denounces the notion.

Among religious sects that do espouse reincarnation, the time between lives (in as much as we as humans understand time) can be immediately upon leaving this life, or up to 49 days. Other spiritual estimates, some based upon documented readings of people speaking to subjects under hypnosis, can range from months to years. I myself have downloaded much of my knowledge of reincarnation, including what happens in between lives, under hypnosis. I'll share a lot of that information with you in the pages that follow.

After a constricted childhood growing up in the Mormon church, I've been doggedly focused as an adult on seeking a wide expanse of spiritual information to guide my own life and help others carve out paths aligned with their happiness, abundance and soul's purpose. I am a teacher and practitioner of tarot and a palmist who has read thousands of hands over the past 20 years. As noted in my first book, Stories in Your Hands, neuroscientists have confirmed that the brain is more closely connected with the hands than with any other part of the body, mimicking neural pathways that actually change over time. We will talk about this concept, which is one aspect of the study of epigenetics — the study of how behavior and environment actually alter our genes — throughout sections of this book.

So why my focus on abundant living? Primarily because we are living in a chaotic and complex world to a degree that our generations and all of those who lived before us on this planet have ever seen or imagined. Because esoteric wisdom including hand analysis is a complex science not readily accessible to many of us, and because I am blessed to be sourced with information beyond typical mediums, I feel it's time to take some stories out of our hands and share realities outside of our three-dimensional perceptions so that we can live more fully.

Abundance is more than just making more money, by the way. True abundance includes perfect health, living in a pleasant and safe home, sharing laughter and joy with family and friends, doing work that is fulfilling and being able to enjoy activities that interest you. I also think of true abundance as being in alignment with your soul's agenda and your purpose in life. Because if you're not, there will be an undercurrent of dissatisfaction or emptiness in your heart. You will have a longing or feeling like something is missing. Plus all of this ties together with your spiritual evolution, your ascension, which we will be talking about in greater detail throughout this book.

My angelic guides would also like us to realize how our modern world is not "reality." By its very design, it keeps us restricted and unaware of our true nature as Divine Beings and greatly restricts spiritual growth.

Here is a message I received from the angelic realm:

We are your angelic team. We are always with you and are happy to guide you when you invite us in. Your world is structured to keep you in restriction when you look at the things other humans have created. You can look at all facets of "modern man" and see this is where you have struggle. Look at the calendars and how they've changed to Daylight Savings Time, the school system and how it teaches you to memorize rather than question or challenge. Even the act of writing is disappearing. The church is a major human construct, not one that empowers but one that disempowers. The money system is also one of disempowerment. It forces you to focus on survival and competition rather than spirituality and expansion.

Many great thinkers have been silenced and restricted all to keep you in a construct that prevents growth of your soul and spiritual awakening. The lost arts and how they have been pushed aside as insignificant or even worse, dangerous or blasphemous. Yet these ancient arts are the way to set you free. Look at the medical system and how it is hijacked and not in your best interest. It is time to get back to your roots that lie very deep in your history. That which is still part of you. Look at prayers and by their design are to teach you smallness and how they teach you to feel guilty and insignificant. No wonder the world is where it is.

It is time for everyone to become A.W.A.R.E.: Awaken Within All Real Energies. That of your Divine Self, not the twisted human constructs from the lower self of ego and pain, the not-self. It is time to recognize the truth of your modern situation, the truth that those who seem to be benevolent are really just coming from the not-self for self-serving benefits.

Soul training is recognizing these shackles. Anything that keeps you feeling powerless, unworthy, guilty and in sorrow should be questioned. One of the goals of this book is to help you to free yourself from the damaging bondage and shackles that have been firmly placed inside the realm of the subconscious mind so you can break free and recognize your true divine nature, which is aligned with abundance.

Think of the vast wealth of information we gather in a single lifetime, and the possibility of enhancing that with truths we may learn after we die and before we are reborn. We all come in with a clear slate, void of conscious memory beyond this particular round, but open on some levels of our being to remember. I hope to ignite some of those memories in order to enhance our current lives—in our work, relationships, and individual levels of self-love and peace of mind. (I will talk more later about how I am blessed with information from light-beings and other entities.)

So think of this book as an invitation to reconnect with your divine nature so that you can live more multidimensionally and manifest anything you desire into your physical realm. We will discover how this inner power is connected to our own process of ascension—or the path of our growth as spiritual beings—and generated by our connection with the Cosmic Heart, or the infinite love that aligns us to the blessings bestowed by the Universe. We'll begin our exploration into these concepts in chapter one and ground them into our innate understanding as the adventure unfolds.

I invite you to explore a field of ideas that are or may be true, designed to open and expand our perceptions of ourselves and this particularly unique world we live in now. One forever changed by events in social, climate, health, financial, and political arenas that even after the past few years continue to move and morph with astounding speed and consequences for us all. There is nowhere to run, nowhere to hide – except perhaps into new waves of wisdom and understanding that can counteract our feelings of powerlessness with equal degrees of freedom, confidence and personal growth. As a spiritual mentor and student of modern mysticism, I am intent on helping each of us breathe easier, manifest our dreams and live our highest potential as multidimensional beings of light.

# INTRODUCTION

If you're like me, you want to live a life that's fulfilling, empowered and fun. You may also want to help others, make a real difference in this world and grow in your spiritual path. To truly create all of that and more, you need to become good at manifesting. Manifesting is more than simply creating. Manifesting is also more than praying, although on the surface they may seem very similar. Multidimensional manifesting is a responsibility to bring something into form from the realm of creation that is in alignment with your Higher Self and the Divine. It connects you to your divine nature and can not only make your life much more fun and fulfilling, it can blaze a pathway so powerful that others will see you as truly magical. Manifesting includes many types of things. Beyond money or material objects, you can manifest things like better health, peace and tranquility, a new assistant, ideas or solutions to problems that you're having, increased intuition, or being able to hear your angels and spirit guides. The list is really only limited by your own imagination.

My spirit guides told me this about manifesting:

> You are already a magical manifester of any abundance that is in alignment with your vibrational resonance. To bring something new into your life, you need to create your desire in the realm of creation, feel it with your connection to the Cosmic Heart and follow through with proactive steps as you know your desire is arriving.

We are going to explore the concepts of this profound message throughout this book.

I was rather shy as a child, preferring to play by myself and not getting into too much trouble. I believed in Santa Claus, unicorns, angels and magic. I remember I used to have a poster of a unicorn on my wall for many years, pure white and majestic, to remind me of this magical realm long forgotten. As I grew up, I forgot about these things and became "practical." It wasn't until many years later that I started to relearn what it means to believe in magic and miracles again. It seems like life just wears us down, we need to study math and reading, we need to memorize answers for a test, we need to get a job, make a living, get married, take care of everyone else but ourselves and continue to be "practical."

I first really learned about meditation when I was in high school, so I guess I was about 15 years old. I remember this clearly because it was not a meditation class that I was taking: it was accounting. What an unlikely place to first learn about something that would become one of the most important practices in my life! Mr. Pavlish was an excellent teacher. He actually made accounting fun and partly influenced me to go into business in college. However, what I remember most about his class was not learning how to balance a ledger. What I remember most were the Friday afternoons toward the end of class when everyone was instructed to lie down on the floor under our desks and close our eyes. This was the first time I ever meditated.

Mr. Pavlish took us through breathing techniques, slowing our breath down, feeling and becoming aware of our own bodies and practicing intentions. He took us through guided meditations and how to look at ways to create a life we wanted, to give us confidence and self-esteem, things that are sorely lacking in the competitive world of school most of the time. It started me down a path of spirituality, one that has led me away from formal religion and control.

Growing up in Salt Lake City, Utah, I was like most people who were raised there. I started out in the Mormon church, the church of Jesus Christ of Latter-Day Saints. I had to go to primary when I was very young, then mutual in my junior high school days. A part of me recognized the patriarchal restriction of this religion. Roles of men and women are clearly defined and there were things I was not allowed to do.

It all seemed so restrictive, with lots of rules where most of the time you ended up feeling guilty for being a "sinner" or just being completely inadequate because you're just human. Or even worse, female. Women are clearly the second-class citizens in the Mormon church. I also was not keen on the constant barrage of pressure to marry and have lots of children. I didn't want to have children, yet this seemed unacceptable in the Mormon church. After all, having children means having instant new members of the church. It keeps it all going, like a business. It turns out that there are very good reasons for me not wanting to have children, including a past life I had in China that I will share with you later on in this book. These ideologies pushed me further and further away from the church, until eventually I left altogether. Interestingly, it was around the same time I was learning to meditate in my accounting class with Mr. Pavlish.

Sometimes we get a glimpse into the magical, the mystical, the realm of infinite possibilities. Once we find it again, we realize that we want to stay there, explore it, expand it. To find a different way to be, to reconnect to what we already know in our heart to be true, but had somehow forgotten it. Somehow it eluded us. We got distracted. I call them weapons of mass distraction and they are good at keeping us from realizing who we really are and why we chose to come to this planet. We'll get into that later.

The purpose of this book is to share with you stories and transmissions from my channelings that will open and activate your own abilities as a powerful co-creator so that you can manifest abundant living, not only for yourself, but for those you love and the greater planet too. Because we are all on a path of ascension, the time is now to remember our divine nature and live the life that we chose before coming to Earth — and that we choose everyday with our free will in the power of the present. To find your own mojo and embrace it in all areas of your life.

This is not going to be a get rich quick book, although incorporating the concepts of this book could activate some new money abundance for you, especially if you set that intention for yourself. This is not going to be a story of how I died and came back, although I do find those stories to be some of the most interesting to read. This is also not going to be a religious dissertation trying to convince you that you must think a certain way or you'll be going to hell (which I've been told many times). This book is going to include what happens BEFORE we are born and all the things we forget when we go through the veil of amnesia, and the importance of remembering our multidimensional selves. Why is that so important? Because it helps us to remember our true power, which lies inside of each one of us. **Life doesn't happen TO you, it happens THROUGH you.**

For those of you who may still be unsure of

whether or not we even have past lives, I highly recommend reading material on Edgar Cayce, the sleeping prophet who died in 1945 and did thousands of readings for people while he himself was in hypnosis. Or read the work of Dr. Brian Weiss or Dolores Cannon. There are thousands of case studies to verify the existence of past lives. I was lucky enough to read the book by Gina Cerminara called Many Mansions when I was about ten. It introduced me to the life of Edgar Cayce and reincarnation. Based upon the evidence of thousands of people, it turns out that we don't just live one life and that's it. We're not "one and done." We live thousands of lives, we just forget them when we come back through the veil of amnesia.

I am interested in sharing with you a better understanding of how our lives actually work, how manifesting actually works. I'm interested in assisting you in taking charge of your mojo, your Divine Self, stepping on the ascension path, and finding peace through newfound awareness. And most of all, I'm interested in assisting you with skyrocketing your spiritual growth and mastery so you can live a sovereign, powerful life, full of abundance and miracles.

Have you ever wondered about the point of your life? Why are you here? Where is "here" anyway? What happens before you are born? What happens when you die? Are you alone in the universe? If not, who is with you? Do you have a soulmate? Why did you end up in a particular family? Why do you keep seeing the same situations over and over? Can you make your life any better or is this it?

I'm interested in taking you to places you may or may not be aware of. I listen to my spiritual guides and what they tell me. It turns out they have a lot to share with all of us and have asked me to relay it to those with ears to hear. I'm not claiming to be someone so extraordinary that I have information no one else has. The truth is, we all have pertinent information to share if we only take the time to actually share it. Or even think about it to know what it is. That's the hard part. To take the time and actually write it down, to lay it out for others to judge, to ridicule, to condemn us to eternal damnation if it's not the same "truth" as they believe. Especially these days when it seems like division is more prevalent than ever. I've been putting up with this for a good portion of my adult life. I've been developing my psychic awareness. I have had the honor and the privilege to look at people's lives in some of the most intimate and detailed ways. I've worked with thousands of people over these years and I know there is so much more to the story, our stories, than most people realize or even think to realize. You could call me somewhat reluctant because it's hard to shed light on some of the topics I will be discussing without facing criticism. You may even think I'm making it up or there's no way this is real. Which is ok, it's not up to me to make you believe any more than it's up to me to personally do your manifesting and spiritual work for you. It's going to be up to you to decide what to do with the information I have to share. Information that I've been gathering for over 20 years of a spiritually driven life, from a seeker of truth, not a blind believer of dogma. The spiritual path can be lonely at times. Yet also very rewarding. I wouldn't change any of it, even the hard parts.

This book is structured to guide you in understanding that **there are eight essential intentions to manifest anything.** My spirit guides gave me this list after I had been working with some clients who were still struggling to achieve their desires. When you have these eight intentions anchored in your energy field, you create a strong foundation to manifest any abundance. We will be going through one intention per chapter, along with stories and channeled messages to further anchor your understanding. These eight intentions are so important, I recommend that you write each one down for yourself and put the list where you can see it and work with it every day. This list can change your life, especially if you anchor each intention into your own energy field and live your life through these intentions. I will also be sharing a little bit of hand analysis as appropriate, although this is not a palmistry book. However, because palmistry is one of my strong specialties, I know it yields some of the best examples. By the way, I did a short video on how to set intentions. You can find it here on my YouTube channel: https://youtu.be/gzGvsDvXENo.

The message is more important than me, the messenger. As a spiritual being, I've been in touch with the spiritual realm ever since I can remember, even if it was in the background rather than center stage. My spirit guides, angels, Higher Self and spiritual team have told me that a book on this topic would be highly beneficial. Just like everything on Earth is a choice, I am choosing to write this. Not for me, but for you, the reader. I'm already living an abundant, multidimensional life. It is my hope that at least one thing in this book inspires you and helps you in your own spiritual pathway. I also hope that it inspires you to take action, action in ways that can change your life forever, planting you firmly in the ascension path of spiritual growth and development, which begins as you move towards abundance.

My expectations for you include that you will not only become a much better manifester after reading this book, but you will also become much more aware of what you're creating in your own life and elevate it toward greater love and compassion, for yourself and others. After all, isn't giving so much more rewarding than receiving? Let's all manifest more so that we can give more and impact others in ways that elevate everyone. I believe in Mahatma Gandhi's affirmation that "If we could change ourselves, the tendencies in the world would also change." My guides talk to me all the time about words and how our words hold power.

They frequently give me invocations to recite so that I can understand how my word choices create change.

Here's my first invocation for you:

> *I hereby welcome and allow this book to be published and read by millions of beings who shall love and appreciate my authentic and heartfelt work. May each of these readers receive many miracles and signs that it is helping them to transform and be in their manifesting mojo. Thank you and so it is.*

By the way, if you're interested in taking your manifesting to a deeper level, I will be sharing invitations throughout the book for you to play with me and my team, to see what we can embrace more fully and manifest together. Check out the end of this book for more details. Here's your first invitation: if you'd like to join my Facebook community, I have a free private group called "Creating Abundance Through Soul Ascension" where we share intentions, ideas and abundance energy together. I do exclusive livestreams for members. Here is the link to join: https://www.facebook.com/groups/creatingabundancethroughsoulascension.

# CHAPTER 1: YOU ARE MULTIDIMENSIONAL, WHAT DOES THAT MEAN?

## Intention: I Am A Magical Manifester Of Any Abundance.

### Higher Self Activation

*I surrender and consent for my Higher Self to work through me*

*I welcome and allow her (his) guidance, trust and light*

*So that I may once again know and use my authentic and loving might*

*Grace, peace and gentleness are here*

*No more room for fear*

*The time is now to fly*

*To my most high, to my most high*

## BEING MULTIDIMENSIONAL

In our quest for the mojo in multidimensional manifesting we must first understand that **we as humans living in this time on this planet are multidimensional beings.** What does it mean to be multidimensional? It means that I am more than my body, I am more than the skin that surrounds the skeletal structure and organs of my physical body. By more, I mean that I have a soul, I have consciousness that is outside my human form. I refer to this as my Higher Self. I am a being of light and the body is my temporary vessel.

As a spiritual person, I find my own path in life. I don't follow any one religion or one way of believing. Instead, I seek out ways to connect to this multidimensional part of myself. The part that is not just the flesh and bones of my body. I meditate every day, oftentimes twice per day, usually for 33 minutes, sometimes longer, connecting to the master number in numerology representing the master healer. I enjoy studying different ways of viewing the world, especially tapping into ancient wisdom. For example, the Mormon church is relatively new compared to palmistry, numerology or meditation. It was founded in 1830, while other spiritual practices date back thousands of years.

I have tried hypnosis a few times in my life. I took a course on building confidence using hypnosis. I also did a past life regression years ago, but unfortunately did not get it recorded. I remember very little from that session, other than it was interesting and lasted far longer than it felt. It turns out I am easy to hypnotize. I discovered this when I was connected once to an EEG machine that measured my brain waves. I learned that my brain stayed primarily in the theta brain state. This is the equivalent to REM sleep where the brain slows down a bit from the typical beta or alpha states. I often wonder if this is why I find it easy to connect to my intuition.

I discovered the type of hypnosis that was founded by Dolores Cannon, called QHHT (Quantum Healing Hypnosis Technique). I learned that this hypnosis was not designed to solve a specific issue like smoking or drinking, although it could probably work for that too. It is a process that allows you to speak to your Higher Self, connect with past lives or life between lives, and ask questions directly to your Higher Self.

**ENTERING A BODY**

I decided that I really wanted to experience QHHT for myself and get some answers that I was looking for. Just so you know, these are not short, 15 or 30 minute sessions. I spend about five hours with my practitioner each time we meet, carefully mapping out the questions we will be asking and the information I am looking for. This is a deep exploratory process. I will be sharing a lot of what came through my sessions in this book. Here's what my Higher Self had to say about entering a body:

> To make it work, we have to forget. We choose it all. Everything is clear in the Crystal City. The Crystal City is her home (referring to me, the Higher Self often talks to you as a separate person) when she is preparing for a life on Earth. That is the purpose of the Crystal City. It seems like we're separated for a time, but we're really not. The purpose is to learn and grow as a soul. We are perfecting, to become more like the One. We strive to be like the One. We would be distracted if we remembered all of who we are. It's very restrictive to go into a human body, like being shoved into a bottle that is too small, like a genie. Then you want out! There is so much pain mostly from being so restricted in such a tiny space. Bodies are very restrictive and difficult to deal with. But they are necessary. For the specific growth that is chosen. Soul growth, accessing the lessons for each entity. It shows a pathway that is very focused. We become curious and want to experience different ways of existing. It's an honored pathway, helps the Source to grow into more expansion. Helps all of us to learn and grow.

We go through some sort of veil of amnesia before we come into our current experience. That makes sense. Imagine if you could remember every single past life and past experience for thousands and thousands of years. It would not only be overwhelming, but incredibly distracting. Some things are better off forgotten, at least for a time. It helps us focus on the current lifetime and the current goals for each soul.

## THE PATH OF ASCENSION

I came across the concept of ascension from many different sources. **To ascend simply means to grow spiritually, to evolve, to attain a higher vibrational frequency.** From my guides:

I learn the process of the soul's evolution. I learn about the importance of being in a body, it's important to be in a body and have time away from the body. Life is balance, learning balance, structuring balance. The purpose was to show you how loved you are and how much fun you can have while still learning your lessons and getting things done. Not to feel guilty or shameful. Don't be ashamed to be a beautiful being of light. To show her to be herself. Don't be someone else. Be you. We want you to be you.

In order to be you, it is vital that you feel like your authentic self, and act from that place of being comfortable in your own skin. To that end, we need to love ourselves, which is the primary vehicle for ascension, and flows through your connection to the Cosmic Heart. Through a divine process of grounding to the Earth while aligning human meridians to the cosmos, we are allowed to expand into our multidimensionality. Through this process, that can extend throughout our lifetime, we discover many blessings, including an ability to manifest with ease, know our purpose, and experience greater joy and bliss. Ascension is essentially connecting to your multidimensional being which also, in essence, defines the Cosmic Heart.

**My spirit guides gave me seven aspects of ascension:**

1. Opening to change
2. Neutralizing karma
3. Discovering of self
4. Embodying the exalted self
5. Learning lessons
6. Connecting to higher and higher states of love and bliss
7. Co-creating with Source

Let's explore these seven aspects so that we can gain a larger perspective on the importance of directing our manifesting.

## OPENING TO CHANGE

Change is important because it indicates growth. The opposite of change is stasis. Choosing stasis slows your growth and ability to ascend. It's like trying to tell a baby to stop growing, it simply is not how we are designed. **We are designed to desire things, grow, and change.**

## WHY IS CHANGE SO HARD?

There are many reasons why change can be difficult. It's easy to get comfy where we are because it's familiar and our minds want to stay in familiar territory. Some other reasons include:

1. **Only using and accepting the five basic senses** – being multidimensional means that we have extrasensory perception including the five "clairs:"

   a. Clairvoyance – clear seeing

   b. Clairaudience – clear hearing

   c. Clairsentience – clear feeling

   d. Claircognizance – clear knowing

e.  Clairalience – clear smelling

2.  **Ego:** This is our human personality that forgets spirit; while it is important, we must not forget that we are highly evolved spiritual beings of light. I also refer to the ego as the lower self or the not-self.

3.  **Ignorance:** To change means that we need to love the search for truth and continuous learning.

4.  **Too much faith in consensus reality:** Many beings are still fast asleep to their spiritual nature and don't even question things or challenge social norms.

5.  **Subconscious programming:** most of our programming is set by the time we are about five or six years old. This is also when our hand shape forms. If we allow this programming to continue unchecked, change is much more difficult.

**Yes, it IS possible to develop your intuition and extrasensory perception.** While it's true that some people are already gifted with some or all of these, there are many exercises that you can do to enhance these skills within yourself. One of my favorite ways is through the use of tarot or oracle cards. By communicating with the cards, you are connecting to your Higher Self while the pictures on the cards connect you directly to your intuition.

Quantum physics is the scientific study of matter and energy, two fundamental elements of life itself. Recognized by ancient cultures for centuries as interactive forces through which we can heal, change our thoughts, and manifest 3-dimensional realities, contemporary science is now seeing these forces embodied in cellular structures condensed under their own microscopes.

By relying on outdated teachings and habitual, limiting patterns of human thought, we actually deny our access to the new/ancient methods of reaching our full potential and creating whole, happy lives. According to Jewels Arnes, ascension coach and founder of Becoming BioQuantum, when we learn to play out our lives in a field of frequency—shedding old obstacles and beliefs—we gradually release all illusions that we are separate beings, rather than an integral part of one universal consciousness.

## NEUTRALIZING KARMA

Karma is the universal law of cause and effect. It suggests that the actions and intentions we put out into the world have consequences that come back to us, influencing our future experiences. In essence, it's the idea that our past actions shape our present and future circumstances. **Karma is what balances and neutralizes our actions and responses.** What you sow, you reap. "Negative" karma is created when you violate the free will of others or engage in acts that are not love, such as murder, lying, stealing, being mean or spiteful, seeking revenge or being overly selfish. Good or "positive" karma is built up by being kind, generous and loving.

According to my guides, just by choosing to be in a physical body creates karma. They further said that it was inevitable, and everyone accumulates it. Rather than having each negative thought or action neutralize instantly, we balance the negative karmic build-up over multiple lifetimes. For example, let's say you did something really negative in a past life and you killed someone. This event would create some negative karma that would need to be balanced. Rather than having it balance right after it was created, which COULD happen, it's more likely to balance at another time, even in a future life. We live multiple lifetimes to harmonize and neutralize the negative karma that we build up through each life, but we don't do it all at once. We may even choose a short life to harmonize something very specific. When you're in the Crystal City and are choosing your next incarnation, you decide how you are going to experience your karma, what you're going to neutralize and how you're going to do it. Here is what they said:

> There are karmic reasons to choose a body. There are neutralizations that are chosen when you are in the chamber (or between lives). When you are in a body, you create karma. The karma is part of the universal way of being, part of how things work. One cannot NOT create karma while in a physical body, it is just the way of things.

As human beings, **we can neutralize our karma by being nice, being loving, and basically just being a good person.** This is much easier said than done, but even just having awareness around it is helpful. We can neutralize karma when we forgive and hold love in our hearts, think loving thoughts, perform loving acts and react neutrally or with love. The opposite of karma is sovereignty, when we are finally free as a spiritual being and no longer performing acts that create karma in need of being neutralized in the first place. Ultimately, we are heading to a stage of evolution where we are off the wheel of karma and co-creating through love. Imagine not having mean thoughts or performing mean acts during an entire lifetime. This is where we are headed in our ascension.

One of my favorite exercises to

neutralize karma is the Hawaiian process called "Ho'oponopono." I learned this when I was dealing with clients who had all types of anger or resentment issues. How it works is you say the following four phrases as you think about a person or situation you would like to heal: *I love you. I'm sorry. Please forgive me. Thank you.* As you repeat these four phrases over and over again, it softens your heart and helps you remember that this process is really for you, a way to set you free.

We maintain our freedom by practicing forgiveness, recognizing yourself in others and all things, choosing compassionate thoughts, practicing kindness but not being victimized (no one should violate your free will any more than you violate theirs), respecting everyone and everything including the self, and releasing vows from past lives and ancestral lineage — the karmic step is essential to the process of ascension because it raises one's vibration in all the little choices that are made each day. It eases any built up karma back into neutrality and moves the needle back toward the light and connectedness to Source. These actions are similar in some of the other steps, but the motivation is slightly different. Karma takes many lifetimes normally to harmonize due to the lessons that are chosen in each life. This is all part of the divine plan. If one is mindful in this process, it can be greatly accelerated in the current life. Recognize the patterns that influence your actions and reactions, as these patterns are the key to changing one's karma and returning to love.

## DISCOVERING OF SELF

The words above the Oracle of Delphi in Greece are "know thyself." This aspect of ascension is critical because we came to Earth to express a human personality and be a being of light. As a soul, you are infinite light, your essence cannot ever be destroyed. When you came to Earth, you passed through the veil of amnesia, forgetting this infinite aspect of yourself. **You came to Earth for a specific life purpose, unique to you.** Collectively, we come to Earth to grow and evolve spiritually so that we may raise our vibration and ascend into the next higher density.

The process of self-discovery is a life-long process. I recommend the ancient wisdom tools including hand reading, astrology, Chinese astrology, numerology, anything that can give you a new perspective or new insight into who you are. We go through the veil of amnesia and forget, but we are not meant to stay in ignorance forever. We are slowly introduced and reintroduced to aspects of who we are so we can grow and evolve. The sooner and more deeply we can discover who we really are, the easier and better decision-making abilities we can create for our lives.

I have found the science of palmistry, also known as hand analysis or chirology, to be one of the absolute best ways to learn who you really are. **Your hands are a reflection of you in all aspects of your being.** It's extremely unfortunate that most people don't understand this amazing science, or even worse, discount it or call it demonic. It is a tool of enlightenment, it sheds light on who you are, your soul agenda, your lessons, your talents, your potentials. It is truly a gift from the universe to assist us after going through the veil of amnesia into our current lifetime. I will be exploring aspects of palmistry in sections of this book, but they are certainly no substitute for having your own hands analyzed by a professional.

By the way, I have a monthly membership called *The Portals of Abundance* where we do group hand readings and answer any questions you have about your own hands! I love sharing what I know about the hands with you. The Portals of Abundance membership allows you to explore this magnificent science while learning more about yourself. Other goodies include group tarot readings, my latest channeled trainings, and mini-manifestation attunements. Here is the link to check it out: https://cynthiaclark.simplero.com/page/308915

## EMBODYING THE EXALTED SELF

What does it mean to embody the exalted self? According to the Oxford dictionary, the word "exalted" means a person placed at a high or powerful level; held in high regard; or in a state of extreme happiness. Therefore, **to live our exalted self, we need to hold ourselves in high regard** so we can exude that state of happiness outward.

Why do we need to embody the exalted self? To embody our exalted self holds the vibration for others and the planet to do the same, accelerating everyone's ascension. How can we begin to embody the exalted self? Look at ways you give away your power or still have an emotional charge, either with other people, things or events. If something triggers you emotionally, it is showing you that there is more healing for you to do around it. Learn about your archetypes and what they naturally wish to express. Most spiritual traditions acknowledge that humans are characterized by certain archetypes, or universal patterns of energy that are part of our individual and collective natures. From the victim to the hero, the jester to the explorer, archetypes are innate tendencies that influence human behavior. These are also physically embedded in each of us, which I wrote about in my book, *Stories in Your Hands: Discover Your Authentic Destiny Using Palmistry & Tarot*. We are all living the hero's journey. Knowing your own archetype gives you a wonderful framework and perspective on your life.

The opposite of the exalted self is the powerless or victimized self. Explore your beliefs, you are not bound to beliefs. See yourself as a Light Body. You are primarily light. In losing density you are like an airplane that is ready to fly, seeing yourself, others and circumstances as positive. Positivity creates momentum, which an airplane needs to lift off the ground. If it doesn't generate a certain speed in a certain period of time, it will run out of runway and be tethered to the ground. Speaking of flying, my spirit guides told me that learning to fly would help me to access my multidimensionality. After thinking about it for over a month, I chose to take lessons and got my private pilot certificate about 11 months later. That training has taught me many things about life and manifesting. Here's a link to some of the things I learned in a YouTube video: https://youtu.be/LnnK19zkqXQ.

Ask yourself: *What blessing is waiting to be discovered today?*

This question opens the door to your multidimensionality and invites good things into your life. It's definitely a great way to start your day.

Each archetype has an "exalted" or innate quality of expression. When one uses this quality to help others, the vibrational energy of all involved is raised. However, the quality being expressed must first come from a place of love and balance. Otherwise, the expression will stem more from a particular distortion that the soul hasn't resolved yet. This is why you see well-meaning people all the time pushing agendas that are not in the highest good of all and fear or confusion result. Find harmony first!

## LEARNING LESSONS

Why do we need to learn lessons? Lessons are there to help us grow as individual sparks of divine light and to reflect to others so they may grow. **Many of our biggest challenges in life help us to grow the most quickly and deeply.** It is through this pain and suffering that forces us out of complacency to change.

One of my greatest growth periods was after my divorce. I was married for 19 years to my first husband. This was a very dark period of my life and I was deeply depressed. Sometimes when "bad" things happen to us, it is for a reason that is for our benefit. I was given the gift of vertigo and forced onto my back with my eyes closed. This was the only way

I found relief from the constant spinning. Honestly, it was terrifying when it first happened. It was like being drunk without being drunk. This forced me to slow down and redirect. It allowed me to meditate for hours a day. Through this time, being forced to go inward, I learned far more and did so much more healing than if I had just been fine and allowed to continue my regular routine. Always look to the gifts the universe is bringing you, even through the difficulties.

## CONNECTING TO HIGHER AND HIGHER STATES OF LOVE AND BLISS

**Love is connection to what is real, which is Source energy.** When we feel we are connected to Source energy (in reality, we are always connected, but in the Earth plane we don't always realize it) – we are connecting back to our true nature, our soul essence. This is the connection we describe above as the Cosmic Heart. It is the true pulse of the universe. Here's what my Higher Self said about this process:

> Do not listen to the fear, do not acknowledge it, do not give it any emotional attachment. It is through the emotional attachment that one gives it more strength. Yes, focus on the love, light, truth, harmony, bliss. It connects you more to the Crystal City, for that is such a beautiful place. It is such a light. It is so easy to shift

one's attention, but there are many distractions that are trying to bring the energy back down into more density. Keep focusing on the light and the love.

## CO-CREATING WITH SOURCE

What is Source? Source is the Creator of the universe, the One universal consciousness that birthed us into existence. Some people refer to this as God. Throughout this book, I will use the term Source, Creator, divine energy, God and the One interchangeably. Feel free to substitute another term as you read, if it suits you better. Why do we need to co-create with it? We are a divine spark of Source energy, and this energy is expansive and naturally creative. Therefore, we are naturally creative. Part of the ascension is learning to co-create this love energy through our existence. Here's what my Higher Self had to say about working with the One:

You go into the body to learn. When you are in the infinite space, there is a Oneness connection where you are more a collective. When you go into a body, it's more of an individual process. It is a very personal journey, a way to evolve. It is a curiosity for the One. The One wants to experience everything so we choose to have that unique experience to reconnect it back to the One for learning and growing. It is an honored choice. Because you choose to go, you don't have to go. There are many who stay and think it's too restrictive and too difficult. Their growth process is slower, but it's also honored. All choices are honored.

It's so wonderful to finally have a road map to spiritual awakening. Although it may seem like a simple list, putting it into practice is another story, one that is difficult and full of pitfalls and setbacks. Plus, when we think of ourselves, we often think that we are not worthy of such a path. How can we possibly think of ourselves as worthy to co-create with the One, who seems infinitely wiser and better than us? That's where the mojo merges with the power of manifestation. Which leads me to chapter two and the next prime principle in this process, which is honoring the true perfection in ourselves.

## ELEVATE YOUR VIBRATION

My guides told me that you, the reader, shall be receiving a vibrational upgrade as you read this book. My guides will be working with you and your own guides so that you may receive activations. They also instructed an anchoring procedure for each chapter. Reinforcing the mojo of multidimensional manifesting includes focusing each essential intention on the four areas we can manipulate in our third dimensional existence. These four areas include our **thoughts, feelings, actions and responses**—all essential to creating our reality.

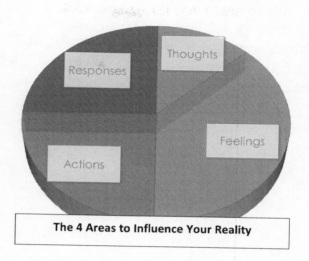

**The 4 Areas to Influence Your Reality**

Take a moment to calibrate your own energy field with these words of power:

> I know that I am a magical manifester of any abundance. My thoughts support this knowingness. I feel my multidimensionality and recognize that I am more than my body. I am taking action in aligning with my knowingness now. I respond to events in my life knowing that I am a magical manifester of any abundance.

### KEYS TO REMEMBER

You are a multidimensional spiritual being of light. You went through the veil of amnesia to find yourself and remember your multidimensionality in stages. You are on a pathway of ascension, a spiritual growth process. Following this pathway leads you to alignment, abundance and soul growth to your next stage of soul evolution, which exists in a higher dimensional realm.

# CHAPTER 2: YOU ARE ALREADY PERFECT

## Intention: I Am Worthy To Receive.

**Invocation to Free Yourself from Perceived Mistakes**

*I choose now to be free*

*I am powerful just as me*

*I release all perceived mistakes*

*From the gentle breeze to the rumbling quakes*

*I welcome and celebrate the essence of me*

*Now all the world is free to see*

*My individuality!*

## YOU ARE ALREADY PERFECT

All of us enter this world as beautiful blank slates, beings of brilliant light. And most of us lose that illuminated innocence within our first few years on the planet. This learned concept of imperfection can have a crippling effect, not only on our overall sense of well-being, but in our daily lives. Many of us have grown up in the constant reminder of Original Sin. We have been taught to think of ourselves as unworthy, wretched little creatures in need of groveling every second of the day in order to be "good enough" to exist.

## BEFORE WE INCARNATE INTO A BODY

Before we come into a body, we spend time in the Crystal City learning from other beings of light and going into classrooms. Here are some activities that my Higher Self talked about before my incarnation.

I go to classrooms to learn. There are beings who teach specific subjects and I'm so curious and am always busy. The classrooms are beautiful. There are geometric shapes everywhere. Different shapes, the shapes hold the vibration for the learning of specific subjects. You go into a sphere, and the crystals hold the energy. This one helps you with your emotional body when you have to deal with all the emotions in a body. It's like practicing before you go in. You can practice happy. You forget. Everything has to be practiced. It's wise to practice first, otherwise you can have a lot of problems like committing suicide and have a lot of bad things happen. There are plenty of

THE MOJO OF MULTIDIMENSIONAL MANIFESTING

resources to practice. You just have to choose. Others don't practice as much. It's more fun and makes it easier when you do practice.

I play colors. There are these streams of color. They are very vibrant. It's like emotion. You move in the color and you transport through the color, you experience it. They all feel so good in their own way, each one is unique. You practice for preparing to be in the body.

**You go through the veil of amnesia to learn and grow in a specific way that is chosen by the soul.** But there are ways to reconnect when you are in the body. The crystals are in the physical Earth plane, they are gifts from above. They are sent to Earth to assist when one is feeling lost, they can help to reconnect to the vibration that was chosen initially by the soul. They are very helpful and want to help us. It's concentration. The crystals hold the power, the vibration, the memories, the keys and codes of all that is from reaching a certain state of development in that lifetime, otherwise they just seem random, rocks, inert, like they have no function. They are given incremental access, it is like going through a series of doorways. You are given one key, then when you reach the next doorway, you are given the next key. You are not given too much at once, or you may become overwhelmed and you will miss the Crystal City. When one knows the Crystal City, one longs to be there because it's so beautiful. Who wouldn't miss that? They long for it. It is through longing that one may choose something that is not in initial decisions. One may choose suicide or psychedelics to get back. They get stuck because they didn't practice enough. It only veils like a band aid because they didn't do the work.

They made an assumption that they could do it.

I spent years channeling messages directly from crystals. If you're interested in learning more, here's a link to a video I recorded on the qualities of citrine quartz: https://youtu.be/W6LmKHOOKYA.

My Higher Self also talked about other shapes and even flavors of the colors:

**Tetrahedron**

There are other shapes – tetrahedron (like a pyramid, but with an equilateral triangular base), star tetrahedron, the Merkaba (or star of David); icosahedron, fractals. The tetrahedron teaches scientific concepts such as

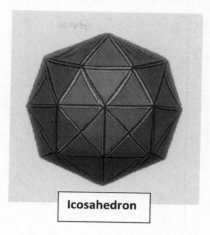

**Icosahedron**

biology or chemistry. The star tetrahedron, the Merkaba, is more spiritual and connects you to the light. It is how you travel from a Light Body to a physical body. It's good to practice. Think of different births, the ones who have practiced come quickly out of the womb. The ones who have trouble in birth are those who haven't practiced enough in the Merkaba. Things are advised, but you have the choice. **Spirits overestimate their abilities in the Crystal City.** I used to do that, but I don't do it anymore. I had some difficult lifetimes and I learned. I have learned to love studying because it serves the One. The icosahedron helps you with navigating once you are in human form. It helps you locate where to live, which job to take, things like that.

**Star Tetrahedron**

Fractals are like the colors, when you are on the ray of color. You can play with the fractal imagery, so much fun! Like being on a roller coaster, but movement in that color ray feels so luxurious. They all feel different, but all pleasant.

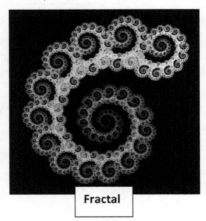

**Fractal**

I love the Violet Ray, it tastes the best. There is a taste to each color. It's sweet, but not too sweet and it also has saltiness too, but not too salty, like kettle corn. Green is tasty, it tastes like delicious fresh fruit, like a watermelon or a cherry, whichever one you like the best. Red is more bitter, like coffee or dark chocolate. Orange is very sweet, a little too sweet for my taste. Yellow is fresh, like a fresh vegetable, like a leafy vegetable. Very healthy. Blue is more subtle. Blue is soothing, like drinking fresh water from a stream that had just come out of the mountain. Comfortable. Indigo is spicy. It's a spicy, hot taste. It's delicious! It's a choice to taste them. I love to taste, it's fun. It's a vibrant sense, taste. It also helps you prepare for going into the human form in eating. When you choose the body and the location where you will be situated on Earth, it's helpful to be on the specific ray to assist you before you go.

As you can see from this transmission, there is plenty for a soul to do before incarnating into the chosen body and life experience. There is no pressure of being forced to do anything. In the Crystal City, you have choices there just like we do here. There may be consequences for not studying or practicing but the soul is always free to make choices, just as here on Earth.

**MAKING MISTAKES**

I grew up as the youngest of four children in my family, not only coming in last, but coming in six years after my next older brother. This age gap created a sense of coming in from behind, a need to catch up and be "as good as" my brothers and sister, with the impossible challenge of achieving it with so many years apart. I remember an early day in kindergarten, where we were asked to draw our teacher as an assignment. Rather than just create a drawing like everyone else, I sat there extremely frustrated until the bell rang and it was time to go home. I still had not drawn anything. My very kind teacher, Mrs. Heuser, came over and asked me what was wrong. I began crying and told her there was no way I could draw a picture good enough to actually resemble her in any way. I was seeking perfection in something that was impossible.

Rather than just give up, she patiently handed me different crayons and told me to draw specific things, like starting with her head and hair, then moving on to her dress, etc. until we had a complete drawing. She encouraged me throughout the process, not judging or ridiculing. When it was done, she exclaimed that it looked just like her!

Mrs. Heuser was an angelic exception to my trajectory of seeking perfection permeated in every class I took. I always worked to get an A and was extremely disappointed if I didn't achieve it. I spent long hours doing homework and going over test questions at least twice before turning it in. I was developing a fear of making mistakes. Of course, missing a test question or getting a B instead of A in a class shouldn't be the end of the world. However, this limited way of thinking robbed me of my ability to just be a kid and have fun. I took life way too seriously and I viewed everything as a huge mountain that needed to be climbed in the just the right way.

## HOW WE ARE VIEWED IN THE CRYSTAL CITY

You are a Divine Being of Light, you just forget and feel disconnected. **There are so many illusions in the Earth plane. There is always a purpose for everything, it is not to punish or torment.** You are abundance. You are the light. You are the love. You are you. You are infinitely valuable! For you are infinite light. You are honored for your choices to be in this body which is difficult. Don't forget your value.

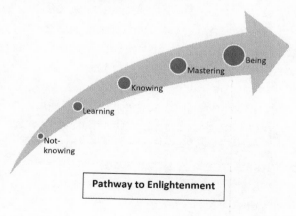

Not-knowing
Learning
Knowing
Mastering
Being

Pathway to Enlightenment

The pathway to enlightenment begins in the place of not knowing. The place of not knowing opens the door to learning, to knowing, to mastering and to being. If you were already enlightened, there would be no need to learn; you see, one must recognize the not knowing, or one simply stays in stasis. Only God is in the place of all knowing, **as a human in a body on the ascension pathway you went to a place of not knowing.** This is the Earth pathway.

## ORIGINAL SIN

Contrary to the popular notion that Original sin is a hallmark of Christian doctrine based on the story of Adam and Eve, the first formulation of a formal edict didn't arise until Augustine's in the late fourth century AD. In fact, Christianity's understanding of the basic nature of humanity is a teaching known as the good creation, quite opposite to the notion that we are born scarred or evil. Christian texts assert that humanity was created "in the divine image, according to the divine likeness," a belief shared by Buddhists and Jews. Islam accepts the fact that the first human couple disobeyed God in paradise, but was forgiven by Allah, just as many of us forgive ourselves and each other for mistakes or hasty judgements. After all, how would any relationships survive at all if we didn't extend a second, third, or countless acts of forgiveness?

Being married to a Catholic for 19 years, I still remember the prayer that says, "Lord, I am not worthy to receive you, but only say the word and I shall be healed." While at the surface, this prayer seems kind, at its core it is not only unhelpful, but programs people to consider themselves unworthy. It teaches them to think of themselves as something far less than perfect and in need of being healed, as though they were born with a sickness that can never be cured, even through constant groveling. Phrases that we repeat over and over sink into our subconscious minds. Is it really helpful to think of ourselves as sick and unworthy of love? In my opinion, church is a major human construct, not one that empowers, but rather one that dis-empowers. By design, the church is in the business of keeping us under control, powerless and pleading endlessly in order to be "saved."

I would love for all of us who still feel imperfect and "sinful" to heal from this negative influence once and for all. If you are ready to heal from Original Sin, here is an invocation that I channeled in meditation:

**I was, am and will always be a perfect reflection of divine perfection.** I release any and all fragmentation of beliefs, validation and assumption that Original Sin is part of my makeup. I let go and admonish any and all beliefs, validation and assumption that I am anything less than a spark of divine essence, here in human form to express a unique and individual experience on behalf of the One, for the benefit of the One and for my own spiritual growth as an extension of this one divine energy. I claim my purity, my worthiness, my dignity and my sovereignty to be free to express myself as I see fit, to follow my own path of light in knowingness that I am and always will be an eternal spark of divine light. And so it is.

I recommend that you say this invocation out loud while tapping on your heart chakra. Repeat as many times as is necessary for you to feel a shift within yourself. It is time for you to free yourself from the damaging bondage and shackles that have been firmly placed inside the realm of your subconscious mind.

## WHY WE SEE OURSELVES AS LESS THAN PERFECT

**It is because of judgment that we see ourselves as less than perfect.** It is because of judgment that we cannot allow ourselves to be at peace with who we are in the moment. When we recognize our divine perfection, we see ourselves as the One sees us: as who we really are, without the human constructs, which are temporary and arbitrary.

It is important to speak to ourselves in our inner voice as love, compassion and kindness. Try to go a whole day without judging and see if you can do it! Look for the perfection in each moment. Ask yourself, **how is *this* already perfect? How am *I* already perfect?**

When you catch yourself making a judgment, say "Stop! I release this judgment now and recognize the Divine instead." Refrain from telling yourself derogatory language, like calling yourself *stupid* or *I deserve that, I'm a nobody anyway,* or *nobody listens to me, why should they?* This incessant chatter of the "monkey mind" that plays over and over like a broken record over time becomes your reality.

## HAND READING, HOW WE JUDGE OURSELVES

Let's take a short detour now and look at our fingers. Fingers give us a tremendous amount of information about ourselves. The hands give us a direct line to understanding our challenges so they may be healed and transformed. Essentially, your hands are direct mirrors to your soul, your personality and how you respond to your environment. I always find it somewhat disheartening when a potential client tells me they don't want to hear anything "bad" from a guidance session. If we are unwilling to look at our challenges, how can we change them? And then you simply stay stuck where you are. Instead of seeing the hands as simply a predictor of the future, good or bad, I would like to reframe your thinking of the hands as an incredibly accurate and specific guidance tool for your own personal growth and development.

Here is a short summary of the names and meanings of the fingers.

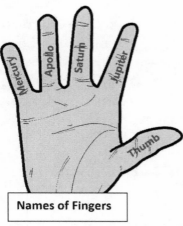

**Names of Fingers**

**Thumb** – Represents your willpower and ability to manifest. A person with a longer, bigger thumb has more willpower and greater capacity for achieving results.

**Jupiter**, index or pointer finger – Represents your mirror, how you see yourself. Someone with a long, thick Jupiter finger takes the time to self-evaluate.

**Saturn**, middle finger – Represents your attitude toward work, duties and responsibilities. A person with a long, thick Saturn finger tends to be more serious and task-oriented.

**Apollo,** ring finger – Represents your creativity and outward expression, how you show yourself to others. Someone with a long and thick Apollo finger is typically very creative, but unaware of deeper truths or potentials.

**Mercury**, little finger – Represents your communication in all of its forms. A person with a long, thick Mercury finger is curious and a gatherer of information.

How we judge ourselves shows up in several ways in the hands, and crooked fingers are a common one, especially the Jupiter finger. It really is much more common to see some bent or twisted fingers than all straight fingers. Your fingers represent different aspects of yourself. Take a look at your own Jupiter finger. Is it standing up tall or does it seem to topple over? Is it thin relative to the other fingers? Thinness weakens the quality of the finger. Both of these indicators show a stress in how you perceive yourself.

How about its length? If Jupiter is more than ½ centimeter shorter than your ring finger, Apollo, it indicates that you don't see or recognize all that you are. You may lack self-awareness and overcompensate in other ways, typically by putting on a good face with an air of confidence. But it's the inner dialogue that matters most. Pay close attention to how you talk to yourself.

If you're interested in learning more about how to read hands, I offer several courses in palmistry. You can learn more about my palmistry and tarot training at https://www.palmistrytarot.com/training.

## GUILT

**Guilt is another common reason that we see ourselves as less than perfect.** This is an extension of judgment. Guilt is the shadow side of personal integrity, a feeling that we did something wrong and feel powerless to "make it right" again. If you catch yourself apologizing a lot, this is a sure sign that you feel guilty.

My Higher Self told me that I had abused my power in a previous life and that was partly why I chose powerlessness as one of my life lessons in this life. It was to balance my karma with power domination and power struggles.

**Dreams are one way to determine our past and past lives.** I had a dream a while back where I was invited into an elevator with one of my male friends. We went down what seemed like miles inside this building. We went all the way to the bottom floor and got out of the elevator. My friend guided me a room that held a beautiful, shiny, solid gold necklace.

He picked up the necklace and put it around my neck, telling me that it belonged to me and it was time to put it back on. Before we went back up in the elevator, we stopped in another room, which was full of belongings, where my mom was sitting. We asked her if she wanted to come with us and she said no. So we left her there and got in the elevator to go back to the top.

Dreams are oftentimes messages from our Higher Selves to show us something from our past or past lives or something that is healing or needs to heal. **Our Higher Self wants us to grow and evolve spiritually.** Dreams communicate in symbols and symbolism, just as tarot cards do. Everyone in the dream is an aspect of yourself. Going down in an elevator is descending into the past. The necklace had a distinct "Egyptian flavor" to it. My impression of this dream was that I had a past live in Egypt where I abused my power in some way and had to give it up for a time. This is why the necklace was locked up in a room. My male friend represented the masculine side of myself, the side associated with power. He was telling me that I had given up my power long enough and it was time to take it back, but this time I was ready to use it in a more balanced and positive way. I think my mom staying behind associates how I may have abused that power and by her staying there, I was not going to repeat the same lesson.

Here's an invocation to release guilt around power abuse:

*I release any and all guilt over any abuse of power I have exercised in any lifetime. I release it to the Divine as I allow forgiveness to set me free permanently in all timelines, and in all dimensions, I hereby reclaim my power, that is my birthright as a Divine Being of Light. Thank you, and so it is.*

I recommend that you take time to analyze your dreams. Write them down in a journal next to your bed and write down everything you can remember as soon as you wake up. This way you will have a record and can go back and review them later. It's also amazing how many details you forget shortly after waking up. Details may have significance and can help you understand something better or give you solutions in your life to help you move forward.

## ELEVATE YOUR VIBRATION

Let's focus on the essential intention of being worthy to receive and calibrate it to our thoughts, feelings, actions and responses. Here are some power phrases for you to align with in your own energy field: *I know that I am worthy to receive any abundance. I feel worthy to receive as I gladly accept the blessings that come into my life. I take action on my own behalf, knowing that when I take care of myself I am fulfilling my divine purpose. I respond to my circumstances and situations knowing that I am worthy to receive any abundance.* Here's a link to a video to see how well you can receive: https://youtu.be/BCK1vjKdDCQ.

## KEYS TO REMEMBER

Don't mistake being perfect as a way to feel or act superior to others. Everyone is equal in the eyes of the Creator. We are all equal, regardless of race, financial status, gender, country of origin, talents or skills. Wouldn't it be amazing if we remembered this truth? To actually see everyone as divine perfection? That doesn't mean everyone's actions are divine, which we'll talk more about in chapter 4. We have free will to choose things that create more karma or free us through love and compassion. Intent is key to everything. Be kind to others who are also afraid of making mistakes or who seem to be making them in your opinion. Everyone has a right to their own free will and their own divine path. It is not always for us to interfere. Keep a dream journal and track your dreams.

Don't be afraid to live and do things that may one day not work out. This is all part of the divine path of growing and expanding as a being of light. Isn't it better to take risks in life and truly experience rather than stay safe behind the side lines and watch other people play? If you're afraid of making a mistake, take a hard look at how you are judging yourself. Let go of being overly critical, especially of yourself. Your efforts are enough. You are enough right now in this moment. If you think you are making a mistake, stop and look at your actions. Strive to be more loving and compassionate, but don't let judgment or guilt cripple you into staying stuck. You are not meant to stay stuck forever.

# CHAPTER 3: YOU'RE NEVER ALONE, REMEMBER TO CALL ON YOUR SPIRITUAL FRIENDS

## Intention: I Trust This Is Happening For Me.

### Invocation for Support
*I rid myself of feeling fear*

*That no help is here, no help is near*

*Support and love surround me now*

*Soon I will be saying "wow"*

*All my dreams are coming true*

*There is no more need to feel blue*

All of us sometimes feel alone. Whether in company or not, we often feel our inner world is shut tight, while the truth is we have cosmic customer service open to us 24 hours a day, seven days a week. How amazing is that? The only sad thing is that most of us don't take advantage of this incredible resource. Even I occasionally forget and make things harder than they need to be.

The reason why we probably forget about our cosmic friends is due in part to our own free will. Because we live here on Earth, we have free will to do or not do whatever we like. And this can't be violated by the higher dimensional realms unless we are in mortal danger. Therefore, we need to invite these benevolent beings into our lives to assist us, to guide us or inspire us.

## SPIRIT GUIDES

**Spirit guides are guides on the other side who work with us** while we are in human form and before our birth in the Crystal City preparing for our next life. They too go through incarnations just as we do, but not all on the same timelines as you. For example, you could have a spirit guide with whom you had multiple past lives with, but he or she decided to stay in spirit form to assist you with your current life. Or it could be someone close to you, such as a parent or child who passed during your life and is now working with you on the other side.

I have also personally had various guides come in for specific learning, such as writing guides or problem-solving guides. You can also call in anyone, living or dead, to assist you with any question or issue. For example, during the writing of this book, I chose to call in Dr. Wayne Dyer, who passed a few years ago and was a very successful writer in his living years. I never met him or knew him personally. In meditation, he told me to keep writing and to keep speaking with the Pleiadians because they are my mentors and will give me information that I won't get anywhere else. He also told me to keep working with the information in the hands, and that I would have multiple books, not just this one. He even offered to help me find my audience, since many of them were also aligned with him. I found this message to be very helpful and comforting.

Before we come into our body, we work with guides in the Crystal City. This is what my Higher Self said about it:

**There are guides for everything.** There are different specialties, just like on Earth. There are specialist guides and beings of light who have perfected their curiosity. You learn from them. You get assigned different guides based on your interests and requirements, it's all perfectly balanced. It doesn't feel like any time, there is no rush here. There is no hurrying, no being late, no missing out. You never feel that in the Crystal City.

The Crystal City is accessible through astral travel. It is recommended to assist with the difficulties in dealing with the Earth plane. Connect to the city when they sleep, they can choose to go back. They can connect through meditation, hypnosis, deep relaxation, guided meditation. The benefit is to remember your light, your infiniteness. Remember how beautiful and immense your light really is. One forgets when they are in the "bottle."

## ASCENDED MASTERS

Ascended masters are people who have lived on Earth in human form, but have ascended already to their next dimensional plane of existence so they no longer are on the wheel of karma in need of continuing lifetimes in our third dimension. They are the ones we look up to in many of our religions. These include beings such as Jesus, Buddha, Kuan Yin, Kali, the saints, etc.

## ANGELS

Angels are similar to spirit guides, except that they do not incarnate in human form and go through lifetimes like we do. They remain in the spiritual realm. Just like spirit guides, though, many of them have specialties or specific assignments in how they work with us. For example, everyone has a guardian angel. This angel is assigned to you throughout your life. They are there to protect you and keep you safe so that you don't die before it's your time. Think of all the "close calls" you may have had during your life and how you were magically protected.

I like to call on my "parking angels" when I'm out and about driving. My husband would agree with me that I always seem to get a great parking space no matter how busy or unlikely it might seem. It's always amazing to me how our angels want to help us in so many ways, even in our everyday mundane tasks. Try calling on your own parking angels and see what happens!

## ARCHANGELS

The archangels also work with us here on Earth and oversee the angels and are not assigned to specific individuals. They help all of us on the planet. Archangels have tremendous gifts and specialties.

They are happy to work with us when we call on them. I personally love to work with the archangels, they have such a positive and uplifting energy and they have helped me so much during my lifetime.

Speaking of close calls, I was driving back from Salt Lake City to Aspen by myself a few years ago. I don't normally feel prompted to pray, usually I just go about my day. This particular day was a good day to drive, it was a weekday and the weather was clear. There wasn't a lot of traffic. However, I felt prompted to pray to Archangel Michael for protection, so I called him in and asked for it. About two minutes later, there was a car moving in the opposite direction that was passing another truck. It was in a no-passing zone so it came into my lane. We were both travelling about 70 miles per hour and I did spot him coming toward me so I began to slow down. It didn't take me long to realize that he didn't have enough room to make the pass before running into me. We were about to have a head-on collision! I thought this might be the end of my life, a thought that passed through my mind in a flash. I was incredibly scared. Normally in this situation, it would be prudent to turn your car to the right, toward the side of the road. However, someone moved my steering wheel to the left, toward the centerline of the highway and this is what saved my life that day. The other car ended up on my right side and stopped in the ditch. My car ended up missing both him and the truck on the other side of the highway. I felt incredibly lucky to be alive and unscathed and I knew at that moment that archangel Michael was with me and prevented a fatal car accident. To this day, I am much more alert on two lane highways and always thankful that my life didn't end that day.

In one of my meditations, I was told that archangels are associated with different numbers. Numerology is something that has fascinated me for many years. Numbers, like everything else, hold a vibration and affect each of us in various ways. For example, everyone has a birth path number based on their birth date. Let's say you were born July 10, 1986. You would add up your birth date and then reduce the numbers to a single digit to discover your birth path. For this birthday, you would add 7 (for July) + 1 + 0 + 1 + 9 + 8 + 6. This equals 32. You then take 32 and reduce it to one number. 3 + 2 = 5. So the number five would be your birth path number and archangel Uriel would be your primary archangel. I will give you a short summary of the nine primary archangels number associations and some of their specialties.

1 – **Metatron** removes blocks, clears chakras and purifies energy. He assists – Metatron's name means "Lessor Yahweh." He works with you, especially when you are a child. He assists you throughout your life with your transitions

in time-space and moving between dimensional realms.

2 – **Haniel** – Haniel's name means "Grace of God." She helps you to develop your intuition, to go inward and heal heartbreak or emotional pain. She works closely with the moon cycles.

3 – **Michael** – Michael's name means "He who is like God." He helps with protection of yourself, your vehicle and your belongings. He also offers guidance in your life purpose and cuts fear from your path. Call on him whenever you need something repaired, especially electronics.

4 – **Raziel** – Raziel's name means "Secrets of God." Call on him if you need help with accessing the Akashic Archives or need spiritual truth. He assists in neutralizing karma and healing past life traumas and vows.

5 – **Uriel** – Uriel's name means "Fire of God." She brings in comfort during times of change, to be the light in the darkness. Call on her when you need a quick solution or epiphany.

6 – **Raphael** – Raphael's name means "God heals."

He assists with all types of healing and pain management, for yourself or your pets. He also helps you when you're traveling, to make the trip go more smoothly. It is said that Raphael is the archangel most often to appear in human form.

7 – **Chamuel** – Chamuel's name means "He who sees God." Call on him whenever you lose something, he can help you find it. He also helps you to understand connections to others and brings peace when you're stressed out.

8 – **Jophiel**_– Jophiel's name means "Beauty of God." She helps to shift your energy from negative to positive. She assists you in bringing beauty to all aspects of your life including your thoughts, feelings, home and office.

9 – **Gabriel** – Gabriel's name means "Strength of God." He helps you with all forms of communication, including speaking, writing, ideas and negotiations. Call on him for creative inspiration and motivation to express yourself creatively.

## EXTRATERRESTRIAL BEINGS

Not only do we have spirit guides, angels and archangels to call on. We also have extraterrestrial beings (E.T.s) who are assigned to assist Earth and its inhabitants in their ascension path. **Some humans have ancestral ties to specific extraterrestrial beings.** I was told by the Pleiadians that you can identify lineage through the fingerprints. These humans are referred to as "Starseeds." As an infinite being of light, Starseed beings come from other star systems in the universe and have chosen to come to Earth to assist Earth and its inhabitants in its evolution and ascension. If you are a Starseed, the benevolent extraterrestrial beings from other star systems are like spiritual parents. You have DNA encoding within your body that gets activated at the proper time and place for you. Part of my spiritual work with clients involves assisting them in identifying their ET lineage, if they have it, and specific activations they can use to call on their respective ET group.

Whether or not we have lineage with these beings, you can call on any of them to receive messages or guidance. Here are some of the main ET groups that work with the Earth.

**ANDROMEDANS**

The Andromedans are relatively close to us and

are Earth's galactic neighbors, being only 2.5 million light years away. Andromeda is a spiral galaxy, also called M31. This ET group is very gentle and loving, while eager to serve Earth.

## A TRANSMISSION FROM THE ANDROMEDANS

We are the Andromedans and are here to bring clarity and knowingness to you so that you may share more about us to your following. Our main purpose with the Earth is to educate and spread love from the One to those who are able to receive our transmissions.

You are highly attuned to the Pleiadian messages and we honor you that they are your primary contacts to the larger Galactic Council of which we are also a part of. You have identified those who are connected to us and may share the following with them:

You may attune your vibration to receive our love and guidance if you choose to be a vessel in spiritual growth and service to those who are ready to also receive. There is no limit to what we may accomplish together for we hold keys and codes within our DNA that has been shared with yours over eons. It is now time to re-awaken these keys and codes in your vibratory field so that awareness, enlightenment and ascension may occur as you move past easily into your next density. We offer these instructions for you.

For you to fully embrace these keys and codes, recite the following with love and openness in your heart:

I hereby call in and welcome you, Andromedans, members of the Galactic Council, to assist me in the opening of the keys and codes already present in my DNA to be awakened once again, so that I may know and utilize my divine birthright of Andromedan lineage to be a vessel of love and service to assist Earth and her inhabitants to grow in spiritual evolution and ascend third dimensional planetary construct. May this process be smooth, calm and peaceful as I reconnect and remember my divine nature and reason for Being. Thank you and so it is.

## SIRIANS

The Sirians are peacekeepers and guardians of Earth. They assist us and guide us especially during turbulent times. They come from the binary star system, Sirius A and B, which is the brightest star system in Earth's sky. Sirians bring us divine harmony, love and peace while teaching us about the true state of the universe, including its accurate history and origins. Call on them to fill in missing gaps of information.

## A TRANSMISSION FROM THE SIRIANS

We are the Sirian High Council coming to you this fine day to deliver a message to you so that you may deliver it to your audience and they may benefit from it too. Our name, Sirian, can be broken into three parts: Si – ri – an or see the truth so you may advance in your knowingness. We come to help those who are confused or lost in the mazes of third density to show the fastest and most appropriate way forward. We are part of the Galactic Council and have been connected to Earth for a long time. We would like to share a short process with you to light the flame of inspired action for those who are confused or lost.

Imagine a flame, like a candle is being handed to you from us, it not only burns with the purity of who you are, it burns with our wisdom and love for you. Place this flame inside your heart and let it light up your own valuable DNA. Let it shine on a part of your heart that has been hurt or numbed to the truth of who you are truly are. What do you see? Let the flame of this candle show you the way, show you the answer. Say to yourself, I am an inspiration, I am inspired, I am inspiring, I inspire others just by holding my own flame of divine light.

Take your message and let it permeate into the rest of your being. Let it flow out to us, and we shall weave it back to you and through you. We shall weave throughout your earth plane so that your candlelight may reach all who need to see it. Feel the heat and inspiration rising within you now and always.

You may call us in any time to show you this path of fire, to assist you and guide you to action. For you are here as Divine physical beings, each for a purpose much greater than you see or know. Use this symbol to work with this message.

Sirian Flame Symbol

Thank you for calling on us and know that we carry you in our hearts.

## HATHORS

The Hathors travelled through the portal at Sirius and are now settled on the planet Venus to assist us with unconditional love. They were called by a being known as Sanat Kumara to assist Earth, secure peace and bring light and love here to Earth.

## A TRANSMISSION FROM THE HATHORS

We are honored to be communicating with you today. There is much stress and turmoil on the planet now. We would like to alert others like yourself to begin to awaken and share the vibration of love. The more and more of you who do this can create a vortex of love that can penetrate the darker and denser energies that have a chokehold on your planet.

Never underestimate your own abilities to transform and transmute anything to love and light. For you hold the divine within your own DNA. It is your birthright to manifest the light even in your third density bodies. We wish for you to understand and speak more words of power and place these words in your own hearts where they may vibrate out in a symphony of love for all those who are still suffering.

Here is a message to implant in your heart and to share with those who have resonance in their own hearts.

I welcome and invite all that is holding the love vibration into my heart and all heart chambers to penetrate and heal any and all remaining pain or trauma. I release and forgive myself and all others for any misuse of emotional manipulation, for it is all for learning and advancing as a soul on this planet. I hereby declare and claim my love to permeate outward to everyone and everything to be felt and healed too. Thank you and so it is.

When you place this message in your heart, you will create a vortex of love so powerful that you will see evidence in your life that this is Truth. We love you and are with you now and always.

## ARCTURIANS

The Arcturians come from the star system Arcturus, located in the constellation Boötes. They are natural-born leaders and assist us with healing, wisdom and planning our ascension. They are innovative and strong-willed.

## A TRANSMISSION FROM THE ARCTURIANS

Although I do not fully understand my relationship to the Arcturians, since moving to Sedona, I have started to receive regular transmissions from them in my meditations. The following is a transmission I received about communicating to all the ET groups listed above using different crystals.

**Starseeds like you have abilities to connect to various higher dimensional beings through the contact stones.** Think of these stones like telephones, they make it easier for you in third density to hear our frequency of communication. You hear us through the Aqua Aura Quartz. You hear others through different stone crystals. Pleiadians through Selenite. The Sirians through aquamarine. The Andromedans is through smoky quartz. The Hathors is through rose quartz. The same applies for other higher dimensional beings including the archangels and ascended masters. **It is not necessary to have direct contact with the crystal.** You may also simply call in its vibration to your energy field. For example, to call us in using the Aqua Aura Quartz you could say, "I am attracting and aligning with the vibratory frequency of Aqua Aura Quartz." This will bring its frequency to you. It can be useful if you don't have a physical specimen in your proximity. Once you align with that frequency call us in to communicate with you. We are happy to come when called like when you answer a telephone call from one of your friends. It is a pleasurable exchange of information. Please share this with others who may wish to hear one of us as this may help the individual to communicate with more ease.

## PLEIADIANS

The Pleiadians come from the open star cluster, the Pleiades, also known as the seven sisters, located in the constellation of Taurus. They are record keepers of the Earth, according to Western Hermeticism. They are highly advanced in their healing abilities and understanding of universal laws and concepts.

## HOW I RECEIVE MESSAGES

I often get asked about these beings and how I communicate with them. After all, most of us can't see them or hear them, how do we even know that they're there? When I meditate, **I practice a process called "automatic writing."** I usually sit in the same place every day when I meditate. This creates a sacred space that ramps up more easily with my energy. Over time, I can get into a meditative state very quickly, whereas if it's a new location or if I haven't meditated in a while, it can take longer. The time of day is also important. I prefer first thing in the morning or just before going to bed at night. These are the times when our circadian rhythms are more calm and more receptive. I've also heard that 13:30 Sidereal time is also a good time to meditate, but when I tried it, I personally didn't notice much difference than my usual times. Maybe it would work better for you. Sidereal time is a timekeeping system that measures the position of celestial objects in the sky based on the rotation of the Earth with respect to the stars instead of the Sun.

In the solar time system that most people use, a day is divided into 24 hours, with each hour corresponding to 1/24th of a full rotation of the Earth relative to the Sun. This system is called solar time because it is based on the apparent motion of the Sun in the sky. However, due to the Earth's axial tilt and its elliptical orbit around the Sun, the solar day is not constant throughout the year, resulting in variations in the length of daylight.

In contrast, sidereal time is based on the Earth's rotation with respect to the fixed stars. It measures the time it takes for a particular star or a reference point on the celestial sphere to return to the same position in the sky. This period is called a sidereal day and is approximately 23 hours, 56 minutes, and 4 seconds in length.

Since the Earth takes about 24 hours to complete one full rotation relative to the Sun (a solar day), there is a slight difference of approximately four minutes between a sidereal day and a solar day. This difference accumulates over time, resulting in a gradual shift in the position of stars relative to our local time. This is why we see different constellations in the night sky throughout the year.

Sidereal time is often expressed in hours, minutes, and seconds, just like solar time. However, instead of starting at midnight, sidereal time starts at the moment when a reference point on the celestial sphere (such as the vernal equinox) crosses the local meridian. Sidereal time is used in astronomy and celestial navigation to determine the positions of stars, planets, and other celestial objects accurately.

I keep a journal in my lap as I close my eyes and tune inward. I do a practice from Qigong, or Chinese energy healing, called the "Three Intentful Corrections." Qigong is something I have been practicing for over 20 years and it is like a moving meditation. It's very peaceful, powerful and beautiful. It's similar to yoga. The first correction is the breath, I become conscious of my breath, slow it down and let it find its rhythm. The second correction is

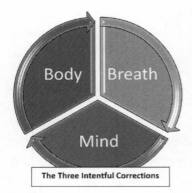

The Three Intentful Corrections

body. I become aware of my body, where it may be holding tension and let it relax and adjust. The third correction is the mind. I become conscious of my thoughts. I allow random thoughts in, but then invite calm receptiveness into my energy field. Become an observer, as if your consciousness is outside of your body.

I sometimes hold a crystal in one hand and my journal in the other. I turn on Solfeggio music or meditation music. I usually set the timer for 30-40 minutes depending on how much time I have available or how tired I am. You can certainly meditate for less than this, anything is better than nothing, but this is a good amount of time to receive a nice transmission or focus on a specific intention. Sometimes I will write down a specific question, such as "What is the most important thing for me to know today?" or I will call in a specific being, or beings. Many times I just do my corrections and start writing.

**Automatic writing is not something that can be forced.** If you're doing it correctly, you will not be aware of what you are writing before it lands on your page. Although I am conscious when I write, I am not in my "logical" brain like I am in the middle of the day. I allow myself to write without judgment or analysis. It works better when you simply write and keep your mind calm and clear.

Whether you have been meditating for some time, or are new to the practice, I invite you to experiment with aspects of meditation described above. You may want to try sitting at 13:30 Sidereal time or choose a time that resonates with one of your favorite numbers. You could set a pad of paper or a journal next to you in case you feel called to download a message from a guide or loved one. Slight variations may alter your practice, enhance it or simply provide a new focus.

## CALL TO ACTION

**It takes more than just changing our thoughts to manifest true abundance.** Meditating on your own may not yield the results you're looking for right away. You need to learn how to anchor the right thoughts and feelings into your own energetic field. If you are interested in my guided meditations and training course that aligns you to all eight of the essential intentions, I invite you to check out my *Abundance Alignment Course* so you can fast-track your manifestations. Here is the link: https://cynthiaclark.simplero.com/page/284847.

## HOW TO KNOW YOU'RE RECEIVING A GENUINE TRANSMISSION

It's common to wonder if a transmission you're receiving is a valid one or not. For many people, it's hard to trust. I used to have this problem, especially if I did a reading for someone who wasn't sure that my transmission made any sense to them. Doubt is a common challenge in meditation and spiritual work, so the higher dimensional beings told me that I could always ask for a sign. **Signs from the universe are an easy way to verify that your transmission is a good one.**

Here's a funny story for you. I was told in a meditation that I would be receiving a sign of an unusual bird to verify the information I had just received. This was not my normal sign from the universe; I typically would see numbers or for many years and roses were one of my regular symbols. I have also asked for unicorns to be one of my signs. Anyway, regarding this sign, it was about three days later when I received it. I was at a dinner party at one of my neighbor's homes, and she had these adorable cocktail napkins for our drinks. The cocktail napkin had a picture of two birds, one with a top hat, and the other with a crazy head dress. It was hilarious! I literally started laughing when I saw it. I stared at this napkin and knew that it was my sign from the universe and that my transmission was genuine. Go ahead and ask for your sign if you have any doubts about what you're receiving. The universe loves to play and interact with you. And it's always a pleasure to receive a message in unusual ways, like with these crazy birds on a cocktail napkin.

**My Napkin "Sign"**

## PLEIADIAN TRANSMISSION

In my meditations, I often receive messages and information from the Pleiadians, since they are my ancestry. The group I communicate with calls themselves the Pleiadian Council of Light. Here is a message that they wanted me to share with you to call them in, understand your true nature and heal from any lifetime:

Here is an invocation to call in the Pleiadian Council of Light:

> *Pleiadian Council of Light*
> *I call you in, a welcome sight*
> *Communicate and share your truth today*
> *So that I may relay what you have to say*

We are the Pleiadian Council of light. We are here to share Loving Illumination of God's Holographic Transmissions (L.I.G.H.T.). We would very much like to share what we can with you and those who are ready to hear the truth. There are many still in the very convincing illusion of separation and agony of distress. We will give you some protocols for you to do to assist in slowly cracking the shell. For if the shell is cracked too quickly it can lead to further psychological or physical damage to the delicate human form. This is why we don't just appear and speak to everyone. There is too much risk and too many still who are trapped inside their created illusions.

"Illusion" – break this word down, I – lus – I -on, I lose connection with the One. It is important to begin to slowly reconnect for all who feel and realize this temporary disconnect and build an awareness of this temporary situation.

## What are the steps to reconnecting with the One?

Step one is to reject the lies you believe to be true all of your breathing days on earth, that you are alone or you are anything less than divine energy in an individual form. Step two is to recognize this in all others. Earth is a playground of choice, a way to experience the physical body and all of the sensations of time-space, an illusion of time moving only forward.

As you reconnect with your true nature you will realize that you can heal anything from any timeline, past or future.

Here is a meditation:

Close your eyes. See yourself as nothing but light, the brilliant white light, like staring straight at the sun, your current Earth star. Let this light go to your infinite past and shine on everything you have ever done or "failed" to do. Let it show you that you are this divine light. All that happened or didn't happen was part of your choice to be an individual expression of the Divine. All of it had purpose, all of it had function, there is no judgment on any of it. Only when we hold on to judgment does it remain in our field and tether us to restriction. Release judgment to be free again and reconnect to the One.

Repeat this invocation:

I release all judgments of what I have done or what I have not done in all lifetimes past, present and future. I am free. I am free. I am free to be divine love expressing through this individual entity. And so it is.

The Pleiadians would also like us to understand their connection with Earth and why it's important for them to assist us. After all, if they're more evolved than us, why do they really care about us and what we are doing here on Earth? I received this transmission regarding this topic:

We are the Pleiadian Council of light. We would like to share with you today about us and our interest in Earth. We are directly vested in the Earth's ascension to also have us graduate to our next dimensional existence. We are not able to advance until you do, for we have also ties with Earth. We have gone through a third density just as you are doing now. **Think of us like your mentors.** It is all an appropriate soul progression. It is a chosen path of soul growth for the One to experience through different selected races. The space-time, dualistic free will energy of Earth is a great pathway not for everyone.

**As Pleiadians we chose a similar soul progression** and are now existing in the sixth dimensional reality. We have deep love and affection for you in your own unique and chosen pathway. We are here to give messages of comfort for we understand the difficulty of being in third density. There are many distortions that seem so real but are not based in the Cosmic Heart of true reality. They are a distorted reflection of experiences from having forgotten one's divine nature. This is one of the hardest lessons to endure in third density, the feeling of separateness from the One.

You must be diligent in remembering that **you are in a distorted reality** and are not separate at all. It only seems so for a time.

Is there a way to help others remember their connection? Yes, speak our truth to those who have ears to hear. And you shall impact many on Earth with our love. **Invite the feeling of divine oneness to envelop you, especially as you sleep to recalibrate your energy field back to a more harmonized vibration.** For there is much needless suffering and it is time for more and more of you to re-connect, especially in feeling, for this is the dominant element on Earth.

## ARCTURIANS EARTH CONNECTION & CELLULAR REPAIR

The Arcturians wanted to share their connection with Earth and the ascension process. Since the Arcturians are known as the builders, they have abilities to assist us with our cellular structure and help us to return to a more harmonized state. Here is another transmission I received from them:

Hello beautiful light beings! We are the Arcturians, here to guide you today in your spiritual ascension. We would like you to know us better so we may be of service to planet Earth, and all who dwell there in third dimensional plane of existence. We would like for you to contemplate our connection to the planet and our race. We chose to be mentors for Earth. It is common as you ascend dimensions to have a planet or small group of planets that you work with, to assist in the transformation that naturally occurs as the planet becomes harvested for its next dimensional experience.

As Arcturians, we operate in the sixth and seventh dimensions, as we too are ascending. We will continue to work with Earth for that is what we chose to do. It is an honor to work with such a robust planet as Earth, full of free will and illusory realities. It is quite different from what we experience. We are especially talented in helping you to structure your experience in a way that is in alignment with your soul's natural affinities. Tell others to **call us in for restructuring and rebuilding especially in times of great upheaval.** Our restructuring may also assist you on a cellular level of your being. Would you like to know more? Yes, **there have been many nefarious experiments done to you** which has resulted in damage to your cells and their ability to recognize its magnificent reflection of divine perfection.

This is why so many of you are still struggling to find your way and are feeling out of sorts. It's like a knowingness that something is not quite right. But unable to pinpoint exactly what it is. **The cellular damage has been spread to the entire world population.** We can assist with repairing this damage if you invite us to assist you to return your cellular structure back to its perfect original state. How can this be done? We can bring wholeness in holographic form in our dimension, and you will experience it in your dimension. Remember that energy is nonlocal. It is also multi-dimensional. This is why it works in our plane of existence to you.

**We have tools and techniques that are currently unavailable to you by other means.** That is something needed for your planet to ascend. This cellular structuring must be repaired. Here is a process for you to follow.

You can call us in this way: Dear Arcturians, friends to us on Earth please assist us in repairing and restructuring our damaged cellular structure back to its original splendor in the image of the One Divine Creator.

Now close your eyes and feel the cells loosening their damaged grip and letting all debris exit through your feet. See the white-gold light enter the top of your head and bathe every cell in your body with its cleansing love.

Repeat this invocation:

My cells are clean, my cells are pure. All damage repaired, all damage done. I hold and embrace the pure light of divine perfection to penetrate and heal every cell within my biological system. My Earth body, my Light Body, all that is me, I am free of all foreign damaging debris. And so it is.

The Arcturians mention in this transmission that nefarious experiments have been done to us. Does that mean that some beings are evil? This will lead us into the next chapter on dealing with "bad" people and trauma.

## ELEVATE YOUR VIBRATION

Let's calibrate your energy field to this chapter's essential intention of your ability to trust. Here are some power phrases that align with your thoughts, feelings, actions and responses. *I know how to trust. Trust is easy for me. Trust is my natural way of being. I feel trust in my heart when I select my manifestations. When I take action in my daily life, I trust that I am moving in the direction of my abundance. I respond with trust in my everyday circumstances because I know that I am a magical manifester worthy to receive.*

**KEYS TO REMEMBER**

Remember that you are never alone. You have an entire host of beings available to call on at any time. These beings can make your life more fulfilling, and they can help you solve problems as they arise. Whenever you feel lonely, call on them for comfort, support or healing. Regardless of your lineage, you can also call on ET groups for guidance, support and higher truth as you go through your own ascension process. Of course, you may also call on the One Divine Creator at any time as well. It is your free will choice.

# CHAPTER 4: WHY DOES THIS KEEP HAPPENING? SUFFERING IS OPTIONAL

**Intention: I Release Any Judgments Or Attachments To How My Desire Shows Up.**

### Invocation to Release a Traumatic Past Life

*I choose to release my past life shadow's embrace.*

*Back where it belongs, in its place.*

*No longer keeping me stuck, I am now free to create my own luck.*

*Recognizing and learning my lessons,*

*Thankful for all my blessings,*

*Shadow be gone, shadow be done.*

*I welcome in and invite the sun.*

Every person and circumstance in our lives is divine but our human perspective often tells a different story. Let's face it, we come to Earth, and we have to deal with a lot of crap. A lifetime is not always full of roses and butterflies. People take advantage of us, we get sick, our loved ones die and leave us behind to deal with it, we get dumped by our partners and left with a broken heart. We lose our dream job, our house gets demolished by a hurricane, our son commits suicide, we get shot in a robbery, we get sent off to war and step on a landmine. **There are so many unpleasant things to live through, it's no wonder that some souls choose not to incarnate.** The pain of being in a body can be more than we can bear sometimes.

In this chapter, I'd like to address seemingly "bad" people, why we would choose a traumatic lifetime and explore the spiritual opportunities and consequences of these choices so we can manifest more of our desires.

## ABOUT THE NATURE OF HUMANS

Here is what my guides told me about bad people:

We would like for you to understand the nature of "bad" people and what their function is on Earth. A good way to think of your human experience is that of a role play. You plan your life carefully before incarnating including having certain personality traits and soul agendas in order to balance karma in a dualistic environment.

There are "characters" who perform acts not in higher vibrational capacities. Sometimes there are even events such as catastrophic events that are caused by one or a few individuals who are balancing large amounts of karma for the collective. This can actually speed up the ascension of those individuals who "die," for it balances their karma and allows them to prepare for the next incarnation where they may choose a more loving path.

**No matter how it may seem, there are no victims on Earth.** Everyone who comes chooses to come and play a role in the growth of their own soul and the impact they have on others. The karma is not balanced in one lifetime, there are many opportunities to pick and choose what to balance as well as the most appropriate form it will take. Once in the body, you have choice to learn to continue to be the "victim." There is no judgment from our side. We simply record and observe. Then when you come back to the Crystal City you get to see and understand everything again very clearly.

Timing of death is also carefully selected for you have already selected the things to work on in advance. Sometimes this may be fluid, such as with suicide, which you know is a possibility before incarnating. The soul being eternal gets more chances to try again. Every moment in the present is an opportunity to be the most authentic being you can be. A good question to ask is **"What is my most authentic expression? How can I be the most me? Who am I in this realm of infinite possibilities?"**

This transmission was comforting because it explains how **suicide does not result in eternal damnation.** My Higher Self also told me that suicide shortens the planned life that was carefully prepared in the Crystal City and does carry karma because the lessons and karma balancing have to be completed, but you still go through a life review and get to try again. The main reason that people commit suicide is because they didn't practice their emotions inside the crystal sphere before incarnating. There is a great deal of preparation that happens in the spiritual realm before entering the body and the physical realm.

## BEING IN A DUALISTIC EXISTENCE

The Pleiadian Council of Light also came in to clarify and discuss the nature of evil acts performed on Earth. This is a concept that many people struggle with. They see God as vengeful and something to be feared. Many people also judge others as good or evil, but this concept is not simply black and white. It's more about one's actions coming from pain and trauma, which could have occurred over multiple lifetimes. This is what the higher dimensional beings describe:

We are the Pleiadian Council of Light. We would like to address the imbalances that occur in the human heart with the Cosmic Heart. Although the Cosmic Heart is always connected and always accessible, most do not know or remember. When there is a feeling of disconnect and there are many imbalances in the human heart, it is easy to see how an individual may choose to perform evil acts of acts that go opposite of love. This does occur in many individuals on Earth and is a distortion that is part of being in a dualistic existence.

Unfortunately, this distortion can create not only a lot of karma for the one performing such acts, but it can also perpetuate much longer than is necessary. For there are entanglement effects that occur in other beings who are around such individuals that results in much suffering and trauma that later needs to be balanced and healed.

When they told me this, it made me wonder if my actions of love and compassion would make a difference to decrease the entanglement's negative effects. So I asked them about it and this is what they said:

Yes, yes, this is an important truth to recognize. **The more love that is held and practiced, the less severe are the not-love acts that will occur.** This is why it is so important to focus on love, compassion, forgiveness, gratitude and service. For these emotions tip the scales back to balance. **The laws of karma that exist are continuously seeking balance.** Your efforts do matter and do change the timelines. This is also why timelines are fluid. There are probabilities recalculating every moment and these can be altered with your own consciousness.

For you are all Divine Beings of Light, even those who may seem otherwise. Simply recognize these distortions and know that karma is operating at all times. Know that everyone eventually finds their way back to the Cosmic Heart, but all timelines and pathways are unique to each person. We invite you to hold more love and more compassion as others choose to remain in the veil of amnesia. Those like you who are awake are invited to participate in assisting with the ascension process. Little by little in each moment, it does matter and does make a difference. Know that you are always infinitely loved and cherished by the One. And no matter what you do, this is permanent.

The actions described in this transmission underscore the fact that suffering, even in the most dire of circumstances, can be averted or lessened – one small action at a time. Every moment presents a new opportunity when we nurture our consciousness and let our awareness expand. It's amazing to realize that by focusing on love, you can turn your whole life around!

## NOT ALL ACTIONS CREATE KARMA

Sometimes we just choose something to have an experience, not every choice creates karma. Here is a transmission about choices:

There are many things for you to remember. The first is that **you came to Earth not only to grow as a soul being but to sample experiences and see how they affect you.** Sometimes you may choose something that is not necessarily part of your growth, or even beneficial for you.

Not all choices carry karma; in fact, many of them do not. However, when you sample an experience and find that you would rather try something else, it is okay to change pathways for it is part of the Higher Self's guidance to put forward another option when there is desire for a change of scenery. It is through consistent intentions where the most co-creation may occur.

To be aware is important, aware of your consciousness and staying aligned and connected with the Cosmic Heart consciousness of the One. This sets you up to have the most positive or pleasant experiences while reducing or shortening unpleasant experiences. A good way to go through life is to check in and ask yourself will this chosen experience result in a pleasant progression or not? Then envision the choice in one month, six months, two years, five years, from the time of inquiring.

## A TRAUMATIC PAST LIFE

When you look at your life from the perspective of karma, actions and responses, it is comforting to know that **you can choose more loving options moving forward in your life.** The first hypnosis session that I did took me back to a traumatic lifetime in China. At first you may wonder why anyone would ever choose to have a traumatic life. But as my guides have told us, we choose everything and everything has purpose. Here is a glimpse into one of my past lives and how my Higher Self described it:

I see a big wall. It's made of brick. It's very tall, probably 50 feet tall and it goes in both directions for a long ways. I'm on one side of the wall. I see trees. I see a road. It seems like the wall is to keep people in and keep other people out, like a protective wall. It's so tall and goes on for so long, it seems like a barrier and I can't go past the wall. I have to stay on this side of the wall. I wonder what's on the other side of the wall.

Everyone says you're not allowed to go over there. I'm not allowed to go. I'm alone. I'm wearing some sort of leather sandal. I have a dress on, it's kind of dingy and gray. I'm a young female, I'm 22. I'm skinny. I need to eat more, not eating enough. I could put a little weight on, I look so skinny. I have some sort of bag

I'm carrying. It has food in it. The food's not for me though. It's for my children, I'm going to them.

I'm walking on this road, I see other people. They look confused. They look like they're not really going anywhere, they're just wandering. Some are going somewhere else, all on this side of the wall. They don't look very happy. I feel skinny, I should eat more. They tell me not to eat too much. They say if I eat too much I will just get sick. I have to keep myself thin so I don't get sick. Oh, they punish you if you eat too much. There's only so much food. That's the problem. They whip you. Everyone is on rations so I save food for my children. And everyone's pretty unhappy. You can tell as you walk through the town, they don't seem very happy. Probably because they're not eating enough.

It's a drought. **There's not enough food.** We're not allowed to go to the other side of the wall. We might be able to get food over there, but we're not allowed. We have to save what we have here and keep what have inside. It's not safe, we'd be killed.

I save all I can for my three children, they need to eat. They're at the house, it's not too far. It's got a straw roof, it's small, the rest looks like brick. There are beds inside. Small beds. There's a fireplace. I have a pot over the fireplace. That's to cook with the food I just brought. To feed everybody. It looks like I've got some carrots and potatoes. Some sort of stew.

I have two girls and one boy. They're young, they're all under 10. My husband is gone. He's dead. I think he tried to go through the wall. He didn't come back. He didn't like being rationed the way we were. He knows that I'm wasting, my flesh is wasting away and he wanted to help me, but now he's gone and I have to do it on my own. He's not coming back. I'm scared. I don't want my kids to starve. I don't care about myself so much. I just want them to be okay. I just deal with it. It's hard. I do what I have to do.

People come to me to ask questions. I help them to see another way so they don't have to be afraid in this reality, which is really hard. I help them to see something else. I put my hands on their head so they can feel my energy. And then I help them to see something else. It helps them to relax. People who are really struggling come to see me. The rationing, some people handle it better than others. I help to calm them down. Everyone is stressed out, I help them to relax and to see better times.

I had a teacher, a lovely woman, she was my mother. She taught me everything. I don't need to be taught so much, it's more like remembering. She is teaching me from the other side. She guides me. They feel better, it's a hard place to live. At least right now. It hasn't always been like this. It's just the drought. The drought has made everything difficult.

The children don't know what's going on. I have to feed them. I protect them. I miss my husband, though. It's been over two years. They miss him too.

At this point in the interview, my hypnotherapist has me leave the current scene and move toward an important day, a day that I considered important when something was happening. This is how I responded:

I see my child dying. There's not enough food. I don't have enough food to feed all three of them. My son is dying, he's weak. He's really weak. I can't feed him anymore. There's no more food. He's not going to make it. I just watch as he's going. He's talking to me. I couldn't tell him. I'm sorry, I'm sorry. I failed. He's gone. I failed him. I couldn't do anything else.

I decide we're going through the wall. Because nobody here is going to help me. And I still have two daughters I have to take care of. And if I don't go through the wall, we're all going to die. There's not enough food. They know it. They just don't want us to know. They're keeping it from us. They're just giving us less and less and less. Everyday. I'm leaving. I can't stay here. I'm either going to die trying or...I've got to go. I've got to go. **I can't stay here anymore. I've got to get out of here!**

I have friends. I have friends who want to go through the wall too. We get together. We figure out how we're going to do it. We have to go at night when nobody's watching. We don't know how far we have to go. It could be miles. That's a long way, I can't see where it ends. But we have to go find the end. You can't climb over, it's too tall. It's over 15 feet tall. You can't go around, can't go under, can't go over. The only way is to find the end.

We go at night. It's hard because I have the children. I don't know what to do, but they trust me. They do whatever I tell them. They're good. We go towards the end of the wall and come to a guard. I don't know, he's just going to kill us. We're not going to make it. There's no getting out. He's so big. I can't fight him off. This is it. We're not going to make it. We try to run away. We can't. We're too weak. We don't have enough food. It's a long walk just to get there.

**He kills us.** Those were his instructions. He's instructed to kill anyone who tries to go around the wall. He has a sword. That's it, we're done. We can't go. Might as well just die. I don't want to stay in this body anymore.

I failed. I should've just stayed. I would've starved. And everyone would've starved.

At the time of my death in this lifetime, my hypnotherapist takes me out of the pain and trauma of that moment and asks me to look back at the entire lifetime and see it from a different perspective. Every life has a lesson. Every life has a purpose. She asked me to look at that life and answer what I learned. This is what I said:

Value the food you have. Appreciate the food. The purpose was to be in restriction. It was a very restrictive life. **Sometimes one has to be in restriction in order to expand. When one is first in restriction, one understands the value. The value of freedom. The value of expansion.** One can fully appreciate the value of expansion when one is first in restriction. This was a lifetime to see restriction, to know and experience all the restrictions in order to fully appreciate the expansion.

Then she asked me why it was important for

me to see this lifetime, what did my Higher Self want me to know and realize?

**She doesn't need to be afraid anymore.** She has all that she needs. She has more than enough food. She has a big pantry full of food all the time. She can feed 30 people at any given time. She doesn't need to worry about things. She doesn't need to feed 30 people. She just needs to feed herself and her husband.

She struggles with failure. She didn't fail. She only thinks she did. She did not fail given the circumstances she was in. That was all she could do. She didn't fail anyone. It was his time to go. **It was her husband's time to go. Her son's time to go. Her time to go. It was not a failure.** She needs to let that go. That it was a failure. She's too hard on herself. **Lighten up, you're allowed to have some fun.** Stop working so much, stop worrying so much, it's ok. If she has a little more fun, it helps to open up her creative side. She gets better answers when she's not worried about it.

She's had multiple lifetimes where she's felt the need to be perfect and she puts too much pressure on herself. This outcome that came through, she couldn't save him. It wasn't up to her to save him. It wasn't her to save him. She thought it was, but it wasn't. It was her job to birth him, which she did. And take care of him as long as she did, which she did. That was what she needed to do. The outcome is not the problem. She doesn't need to worry about the outcome. **The results actually don't matter at all.** She's just the messenger. The results take care of themselves.

The wisdom that I gained from looking back at that traumatic lifetime reinforced in me that every lifetime has a purpose and we choose it all. I chose to have that restrictive life in order to fully appreciate an expansive life later on.

## EMPOWERING EMPATHS

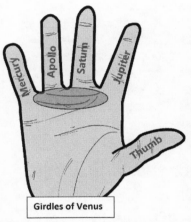

Girdles of Venus

**Empaths are people who are extra sensitive.** Their hands will be very soft, fingers are typically narrow and pointed, and they often have a marking called "girdles of Venus" which are minor lines located just under the middle and ring fingers and look like a half-circle. I work with empaths often because they are also quite intuitive and are usually interested in spiritual topics. Empaths often struggle in relationships and attract less-than-ideal partners, (what I call the "fatal attractions") because they develop co-dependencies and boundary violations.

Here's what my guides told me about empaths:

**There are sensitive types that have trouble for they are absorbing other people's energies through quantum entanglement.** This makes it difficult for them to move forward or understand themselves, for they can easily get jumbled and enmeshed in emotional changes. The reason they struggle is not only an inability to distinguish their own energy field, but they don't know how to clear out and detox their field or the spaces where they dwell. Look at the not-self aspects and lessons and how they play out in all areas of life. Once they become empowered, they will begin to see shifts in their relationships, clarity and abundance. This is also good training for those who want to connect more to their emotional selves to be better communicators and develop deeper and more meaningful connections. This is also where heart chamber healing is so valuable.

## THE FIVE GOLDEN RULES OF RELATIONSHIPS

**Relationships are one of the best ways to grow and evolve as a soul being.** Through my meditations, I learned that there are five golden rules with relationships:

1. Relationships bring soul growth.

2. Relationships are mirrors.

3. All relationships are sacred.

4. Relationships are dynamic.

5. Relationships allow us to embody love.

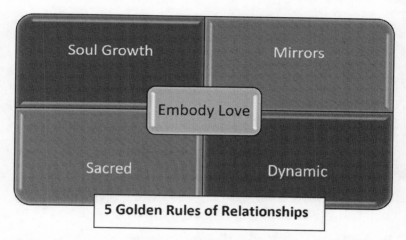

**5 Golden Rules of Relationships**

Take these five golden rules and create questions and concepts around them.

1. How did your soul grow from your relationship with (x)? What did your soul learn from your relationship with (x)?

2. What did you learn about yourself in your relationship with (x)?

3. How is your relationship with (x) sacred? There are no mistakes in relationships.

4. What did your relationship with (x) allow you

to change in your life? How might this have been more challenging or missed otherwise?

5. How is your relationship with (x) allowing you to embody love even more? What did your relationship with (x) teach you about love?

When we go through this exercise, we can gain a higher perspective on our relationships, which builds greater compassion and understanding. Relationships are a wonderful way for us to know and expand love, which is what we are naturally. Even painful relationships serve this purpose, although from the ego perspective it may not seem so. As you integrate these concepts in your knowingness you will be able to see and interact from the higher divine perspective in all your relationships.

If you are interested in igniting soulmate love, healing from past relationships and empowering yourself in all of your relationships, I have a comprehensive course, called *How to Ignite Soulmate Love*, that can assist you. Here is a link: https://cynthiaclark.simplero.com/products/78574-How-to-Ignite-Soulmate-Love

## CHALLENGING RELATIONSHIPS

Here's another transmission that came through regarding negative relationships.

We sometimes end up in certain negative relationships or emotional situations. Look at it from the perspective of the heart chamber lessons. For example, having a manifestation heart chamber blockage is experiencing an emotional failure on some level, which may be in the relationship arena or elsewhere such as work. The soul is trying to show that success is already present regardless of the external results.

**Once that lesson is recognized in the vibratory field of the individual, the emotional blockage disappears.** Harmony is restored and new experiences will begin to show up as a result. Think and feel in this solution energy until the vibration changes. It is important not to let the physical reality impact you because what you experience in the present is simply the reflection of what you believed to be true in your recent past.

**Plant the seeds for your future by analyzing the emotions that are blocked in your heart chambers as the place to begin to create your new reality.** This is also good to do for those repetitive thoughts and feelings brought forward by the collective. Hold the space for others to reach their highest potential rather than the easy path of seeing them as stupid or unable to change. The truth is that change can occur in the blink of an eye. You have had epiphanies so you know this to be true. Hold the space of love for all to come into alignment, even the Luciferian followers. You are gratitude, alignment and purpose. These are the main gifts you are accessing now.

## HEALING RELATIONSHIPS

Here are the keys for recreating harmony in any relationship.

1. **Get yourself in balance within your archetype.** For example, if your hand shape reveals that you are a High Priestess archetype, in relationships you may be naturally secretive. Find the balance between sharing too much and not sharing at all. Please refer to my other book *Stories in Your Hands* if you're interested in learning more about your archetype.

2. **Set appropriate boundaries and expectations.** We may very well get to the point where we are all telepathic, especially as we ascend. Until then, your partner cannot read your mind. Don't assume anyone knows what you're feeling and keep your communication clear.

3. **Follow through when needs are not met.** If your partner violates your already clearly-communicated needs, don't just tolerate it or become angry and hold it in. You are allowed to take action on your own behalf, preferably in a way that is not destructive or creates karma.

4. **Let go of judgment.** It's so easy to judge! This one takes some work. Try seeing the other person in a better light and continue to hold positive expectations.

5. **Don't fall into the same patterns of reaction.** If you keep reacting in the same way, you will likely create the same scenarios over and over again. Build your own self-worth and security. No one else can "make" you feel anything, you have choice, including choosing to be angry and reactive.

6. **Pay attention to repetitive negative thoughts** around the relationship, such as statements that include "always" or "never."

7. **Reiterate your love for each other.** At the end of the day, if you love this person, tell them and hold love and compassion in your heart.

If you are in a marriage or committed relationship, my guides gave me this invocation for relationship empowerment when I was having a tough time with my husband. When I tried this, the next day things got much better!

I hereby claim and declare all codependent and base impulse interactions complete with my partner. I call in and welcome divine assistance in clearing old stories of fragmented pain to be washed and purified. I declare and claim my worth as a divine god/goddess of light to be treated with honor and respect. From this moment forward. As I shall do in reciprocity. I am value love, honor, courage and wisdom full of divine energy to be shared in respect and loving honor as the sacred marriage vow is intended. I release pain, judgment, blame and all past trauma to be healed and transmuted to light now. And so it is.

Read this again out loud before bed and feel the pain lift by morning.

## HEALING THE SHADOW SELF

First of all, let's talk about what the shadow self actually is. The concept of the shadow self originates from the teachings of Swiss psychiatrist Carl Jung. The shadow self refers to the aspects of our personality, emotions, and behaviors that we tend to reject, deny, or repress. It encompasses the parts of ourselves that we deem unacceptable, shameful, or incompatible with our self-image or societal norms.

Here are some key points to understand about the shadow self:

1. **Unconscious and Repressed:** The shadow self consists of unconscious and repressed aspects of our psyche. These can include our fears, insecurities, repressed desires, unresolved conflicts, negative beliefs, and suppressed emotions. It represents the parts of ourselves that we have disowned or pushed away from our conscious awareness.

2. **Projection:** The shadow self often projects its rejected qualities onto others. What we dislike or judge in others may reflect aspects of our own shadow that we are unwilling to acknowledge or integrate. The shadow can manifest in our interactions and relationships, causing us to react emotionally or judgmentally to others' behaviors that mirror our disowned parts.

3. **Integration and Wholeness:** Embracing and integrating the shadow self is a crucial part of the journey toward wholeness and self-awareness. By acknowledging and facing our shadow, we can gain

a deeper understanding of ourselves, heal emotional wounds, and reclaim the fragmented parts of our being. This integration process can lead to greater self-acceptance, authenticity, and personal growth.

4. **Light and Dark:** The shadow self is not inherently negative or evil; it encompasses both light and dark aspects. It includes qualities that society may label as negative, such as anger, jealousy, greed or selfishness, but it can also contain hidden strengths, creativity and untapped potential. By exploring and accepting the shadow, we can harness its energy and transform it into positive qualities.

5. **Personal and Collective:** The shadow self is not limited to individual experiences but can also have collective dimensions. It reflects the unacknowledged and unconscious aspects of society, culture and humanity as a whole. Unresolved collective shadows can manifest in societal issues, conflicts, and patterns of behavior that need to be addressed for collective healing and growth.

**Exploring the shadow self requires self-reflection, honesty, and a willingness to face discomfort.** By embracing and integrating our shadow self, we can move towards greater self-awareness, compassion, and authenticity, allowing for a more balanced and whole expression of ourselves.

Over the years I have helped many clients through all sorts of negativity and traumatic events.

Here is a simple meditation you can do to cleanse the shadow self:

See your shadow self come out of your body and a beam of sunlight shines directly on it. Watch the shadow disappear into the sun's light.

What path leads to wholeness? Here is a transmission about it.

The path that integrates all parts of the self, all desires of the archetypes, especially your own and harmonizing them such that they have the ability to express themselves through your soul essence. You are in a winter cycle now moving into spring soon. In the winter when all is seemingly dead, there is beauty in the fresh snow allowing you to purify your intentions and receive the messages you need to hear in order to be ready when the spring arrives. Your true desire is that all become enlightened, and no one continues to follow and act on the falseness of the lower vibrations.

**What is enlightenment? It is recognition of light. What is light? It is the Divine.** You will not find your path to wholeness by looking outward. You must turn inward and see the light that dwells within you first, then express this light in your life. See the light in all things even those you "dislike" and give compassion to all on their paths, for all paths are divine.

Enlightenment is bringing in more light and reducing that which is not light, or that which is disguised as light but is not really light. Disguises include the martyr, the impoverished, the righteous, the competitor, the settler, the uncurious, the scientist. What personas do people hide behind that keeps them from embodying their infinite light?

## ELEVATE YOUR VIBRATION

Let's calibrate your energy field to this chapter's essential intention to releasing judgments and attachments. Here are some power phrases that align with your thoughts, feelings, actions and responses. *I know how to release judgments and attachments. I am an open vessel to allow the universe to bring me my desires in whatever way is most aligned with my Higher Self. I feel judgments and attachments releasing from me now. When I take action in my daily life, I let go of how my abundance shows up, knowing that it shows up in ways that are perfect for me. I respond with openness in my everyday circumstances because I know that I am a magical manifester worthy of receiving and I trust that all is well.*

### KEYS TO REMEMBER

Every person is a Divine Being of Light, regardless of their personality or their actions. When someone performs an action that goes against love, this creates karma. This karma will need to be balanced in the current life or a future life. People choose traumatic lifetimes for a purpose and a lesson. Great learning and growth happen through relationships. Holding on to judgments and attachments only restricts your manifesting mojo.

# CHAPTER 5: YOU'VE BEEN HERE BEFORE WITH THE SAME PEOPLE

## Intention: I Am Resonating With My Desire.

### Ancestral Heart Chamber Invocation

*I walk the path of the ancestral line*
*Bringing forward what has always been mine*
*Healing, growing and knowing*
*The light of the Divine I am sowing*

When we are born into a new lifetime, we are naturally equipped with two basic foundations from past lifetimes. One is a set of soul contracts with other beings—family, friends, associates—who we have carefully selected to journey with us this time around.

We have travelled side by side with many of these beings before. The second foundation is a broad range of knowledge and experience available to us from past lifetimes. We generally don't remember the people or the talents that are part of our new incarnations, but we are often drawn to certain people's energy, or inspired to use particular talents as we grow and evolve into adults.

Both of these create a resonance in our energy field which results in us attracting similar patterns and experiences over and over into our lives. To manifest something new, we need to resonate with the new, or something we've done before and have forgotten.

## SOUL CONTRACTS

Beyond our nuclear family, we build a series of friends and associates that can carry the same or greater significance in our lives than those who share our DNA. **Some carry soul contracts to share one task with us,** like writing a book, or to support us during challenging times. No matter what the specifics of the contract may be, even and often especially the hardest ones, each encounter is designed to expand the growth of our souls.

Here's what my Higher Self said about this subject:

> **Relationships are forged in spirit, and in many lifetimes.** Not all of these relationships carry soul contracts. Typically, the more important relationships in your life do. And always your parents and siblings are carefully chosen prior to entering your body. But as you also know certain contracts may be completed in other lifetimes, not necessarily the one you are currently living. Many times you may also be able to declare a contract complete, especially if you have already learned the lesson associated with that person. The key is in the learning. Otherwise, you will simply attract another person who will continue showing you the same lesson in a slightly different reality. This is why it is so important to understand the role the other person is playing. What are the dynamics being played out for both sides? **If you die before the lesson is fully learned you will continue it again in another lifetime.** This is also why it is important to look at and make progress in lessons. **Love is always the way through.**

When we speak of love, many of us are coming to understand that the energy of love encompasses all facets of our lives, beyond the single notion of romance. Brian Weiss, psychiatrist, hypnotherapist, and pioneer in the field of past life regression said "Often when the lessons to be learned in the relationship are completed, the relationship has a natural ending and the two souls move on. Also, there are many types of love and many types of soul relationships. Romantic love is only one of these types..."

Of all the ways to categorize soul ties, the popular notion of "twin flames" is perhaps the most interesting. Reincarnation research from Michael Newton, Dr. Brian Weiss and and Dr. Helen Wambach all describe people who appear to have simultaneous incarnations in different realms of the universe— an idea confirmed by my Higher Self in this transmission:

**Twin Flames are a single soul in two different bodies.** As an infinite being of light, you have the choice to divide your own energy for the purpose of accelerated growth. Most souls do not choose to do this. The second body may be the same sex or different, and the timelines of birth and death are typically close to each other but not exact. Before this path is chosen, the soul also decides if the "twin" will meet the other or not during the lifetime.

Most choose to keep them separate for there can be intense emotions that are hard to handle while in a body. It is also often chosen to have each twin work on completely separate pathways of growth, to rebalance karma or have different experiences that are later brought back together in the Crystal City. Only the most adventurous and bravest souls choose this option. This is why it is not common.

Generally, we recognize a twin soul by that instant feeling we sometimes have of knowing someone deeply though we've never consciously met before. That instant hit can be accompanied by strong feelings of love, an energetic pull, or a desire to help that person.

At the other end of the soul tie spectrum are large groups of souls, or "soul families," which can include family, friends, colleagues or people who never actually meet on the earth plane. According to my guides:

**Soul families are other beings on the Earth pathway with similar lessons, similar purposes and similar vibrational resonances.** They naturally develop as you move along through your lives on Earth. Soul families usually consist of several thousand to several million souls, depending on the areas of growth being chosen. Some areas and situations are quite specific, so not very many will be a part of that soul family, while others are more commonly experienced. Therefore, several million souls may resonate with those circumstances. It is common to incarnate over and over with close members of your soul family, sometimes playing out the same relationships and sometimes not. It is carefully chosen before entering a new body and new life. Most of the important people in your life will have worked with you and you will have worked with them in prior lifetimes.

It is not unusual for a member of our soul families to help us align with our desires by igniting our work or callings by sharing a similar sense of feeling or purpose.

## CREATING RESONANCE WITH PAST LIFE GIFTS

The following is an invocation to help you transition into fourth density vibration and calibrate yourself as you make the transition:

*I am ascending to my highest vibrational capacity,*

*I welcome and allow the light to let me see,*

*My essence of being is essential and a*
*precious Starseed delight,*

*Love and glory is my right.*

When we remember that we are infinite beings of light and that our souls are eternal, we realize that **we have accumulated many lifetimes of knowledge and experience.** Wouldn't it be amazing to be able to access some of those talents that you have already mastered in another lifetime?

Before we learn how to tap into those skills and passions, we often feel disconnected, as though you are missing something but you aren't sure what it is. You may be experiencing fragmentation. **Fragmentation is a feeling of separation.** This is when you feel as if parts of yourself are missing or lost. One goes through this to discover what is really important in life. It is a redirection for the soul. Fragmentation easily occurs during times of change. It is the time to ask who you are and seek inwardly for the answers. It's as if our soul longs to connect back to a previous experience or gift, because it was pleasurable or fulfilling.

## RETRIEVING TALENT INFORMATION

The truth is we can also access fragmented information inside of us with the help of various practices that inform and guide us. One of them is through the messages in our hands. Here's what my guides had to offer:

> The soul collects talents from past incarnations. These are temporarily forgotten just like everything else when you go through the veil of amnesia. **If the soul wants you to remember, it may show up on the passive hand** as you have seen, these could also represent as an Apollo line on the passive hand, pay attention to this line and how it varies with the active

hand. You may also be instantaneously triggered by something in your external world. Anyone who has ever had déjà vu will know this to be true. Déjà vu is a form of activation, as is often the near-death experience when one temporarily crosses back into the spiritual realm.

## PALMISTRY, THE APOLLO LINE

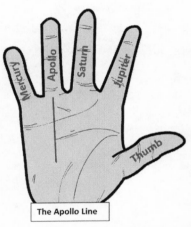

The Apollo Line

One point of entry is the Apollo line on the hands. The Apollo line is a minor line that runs vertically down the palm directly under the Apollo finger. It is also commonly called the Sun line, because Apollo was the god of the Sun. Modern palmistry translates this line as a line of talent representing something that you spend time developing based on its length. The longer this line, the more time and effort the person has expended to work with a particular talent. Some people do not have an Apollo line on one or both hands, that's why it's called a minor line (although if they don't, it doesn't necessarily mean they are lacking in talent). It is common to see this line quite short, ending shortly below the finger. It is also common to see this line in multiples, indicating a splitting of time and effort on more than one gift. For this line, on the passive hand it would show a potential talent while on the active hand it would show something already developed and ready to be used. **This line is often associated with creativity and creative flow.**

**You can also be participatory with the lines of your hands, even addressing them directly.** Here's an intention that my guides told me would be beneficial to say while massaging your Apollo line:

> I am aligning with my spiritual path as I let go of all that no longer resonates with my highest potential.

## THE AKASHIC ARCHIVES

**Talents can also be read from the Akashic Archives (also called Akashic Records).** I first learned about these spiritual records when I read about Edgar Cayce's life as a child. The Akashic Archives are a storage center for everything you have ever done in any lifetime. Literally, everything gets recorded. When you die and return to the Crystal City, you go through a Life Review where you view your Akashic Archives in 360 degrees, first from your human perspective, second from the perspective of those you interacted with and third from a neutral perspective. Then you review the life you just had with your spiritual guides to determine how well you met your objectives. The advantage of knowing and accessing the Akashic Archives while you are still living can be tremendously valuable to manifest in alignment with your soul. My guides told me this about it:

> One could also access these gifts through the Akashic archives and going to your personal Hall of Records. A process would be to ask to be shown a glimpse of a previous life that wishes to carry forward into this one. Another way is through hypnosis or regression, to get information about other times and experiences to help you in the present.

When I was working as a palm reader in Salt Lake City, Utah, I spent some time with other spiritual healers and readers. One of these psychic channelers became a good friend of mine and we spent many afternoons channeling. Suzanne brought forward information that I was a palm viewer and could access the Akashic Archives through the palms. This is what she channeled back in 2010:

> Your heart contains a library of information for palm viewing. You are a palm viewing master from another lifetime. **Palm viewing is a sacred gift to you that**

**allows a human being to read archived information from the palm of one's hand.** This gift will come forward through your speaking voice from your heart and the person you are speaking to will witness that it is true for the witness of truth always accompanies the information from the Akashic library, the akashic record file, the akashic archive. The akashic is available through the solar realm and the golden corridor.

It is interesting to me that after she opened this channel up from my past life, whenever I called on the Akashic Archives to be open and available, I would see golden light in my third eye view. That was my confirmation that it was open and ready to share information. So the golden corridor is like the hallway to walk into when you wish to read from the archives, like the connector.

## OPENING THE GOLDEN CORRIDOR

Here is an invocation my guides gave me along with a procedure to follow.

*I choose to open and reconnect to the golden corridor,*
*I am light and love evermore,*
*Thank you for this blessing,*
*Empowered, calm and no more guessing.*

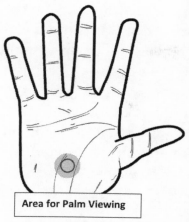

Area for Palm Viewing

After speaking this invocation out loud or to yourself, close your eyes and center yourself. Wait for the golden light to appear in your own third eye. Or you may have some other indicator that lets you know that it is open. Then open your eyes, and gaze at the palm. **This process is not the same as palm reading.** It is more like a psychic experience similar to psychometry where you use an object to receive information. In this case, the object is the palm. Suzanne's guides told me to look about two-thirds of the way down the palm in the center, in between the fate line and the life line. See the photo for the approximate location to place your eyes, although you will not be looking directly. It is more of a gaze, like when you look at those photographs with the hidden holographic pictures embedded in them. I also call this a soft gaze. You may look here on both the right and left hands, then proceed with a question, such as **"What talent or gift do I have from a previous lifetime that would like to come forward in this lifetime?"** Then wait and see what comes through.

**Lemurian Seed Quartz**

**You can also use Lemurian seed quartz crystal.** This is a beautiful clear quartz with horizontal lines running through its body. These lines hold the records of the Akashic archives. I often hold this crystal in one hand and look at my opposite hand for palm viewing when I want to connect with the Akashic archives.

Curious about some of my own talents, one evening I decided to call in my guides and ask them about it. They focused on gifts I have to offer to others, highlighting my own gifts:

Thank you for connecting with us today, we would like to show you your own gifts, so that you may see how to direct them in a way that serves you and the planet. You are a light in the darkness to people who are suffering from spiritual starvation. By this we mean that people are aware of something missing, a void that is not being filled by church, spouse, friends, etc. A feeling that there is more, more of something but not being sure how to access it or be filled up.

Spiritual food is the food of true healing to access to one's divine nature, the ability to finally experience peace and harmony inside instead of hungering to keep eating that which does not truly nourish. You help others to find more deep meaning so they have access to the hidden and dark recesses of the psyche in order to finally be free. Free of things that don't matter, like worry, stress, fear, uncertainty. What can be worse than a life without meaning?

Meaningful manifesting is what you bring to the table, a way to recognize what is meaningful and what is hidden in pain or drudgery. Only that which is in alignment with the Higher Self has lasting meaning. The greatest work is the inner work as you know, but the soul must be able to clearly see the patterns.

## CONNECTING TO GIFTS THROUGH STARS

If you are an astrologer or astronomer with an interest in specific stars, I often recommend that you go outside at night to gaze at the night sky. This is what my guides said about stars and their ability to assist us in tapping into our gifts:

Star energies are also useful to bring forward the specific stars are like crystals and hold special light to be harnessed. The same is the case with the planets and various alignments. Knowing your [astrological] placements can be useful in this life, as well as the transits, conjunctions etc. They all impact each other.

Starlight is apparently very important as well to give us that sense of home. When you think about having a "birth star," then you also must have gifts that come from that star and ancestral lineage. There is even a starlight chamber in the Crystal City you can visit. I would think that if you go there in a meditation, you could also harness your divine gifts from that star. Here is what my guides described:

> What is a birth star? In the Crystal City, there is a starlight chamber that is used to help you recalibrate with your birth star. **After spending time on Earth, you may have a feeling of missing home.** This chamber can be programmed to bring in the starlight from anywhere in the universe and charge you back up with that light. It is very healing to do when you return to the Crystal City and before your next incarnation.
>
> You can access the starlight chamber in meditation to connect with your birth star. You go into the chamber so that the energy is dispensed in the exact intensity that is most beneficial for your personal Being. The starlight penetrates your energy field like mother's milk so that you feel home, rejuvenated and recharged in every way.

## CREATING NEW RESONANCE

**One of the most important things to remember is that to manifest what you desire into your life, you have to resonate with that desire.** You must hold value, as we discussed in Chapter 2. The more value you hold for yourself, the easier it is to create new resonance with your desires. After all, if you don't see your gifts and talents as having value, how will anyone else, including the universe?

Self-worth issues easily permeate into our abilities to recognize and build our talents. Sometimes it is easier to give up before we even start. Does that sound familiar to you? My guides gave me this wonderful meditation to do to build overall value. For 10 money intentions, check out this video: https://youtu.be/oZ9aEd9z1mI.

> To see your value, envision your body as an empty piggy bank, fill it with gold, coins, money, jewels, et cetera from the top of your head. See the items fall to your feet and slowly fill you up until you are completely full. See the abundance overflow around you. Now see yourself bathing and liquid gold absorbing into every pore, every cell. Feel the warmth radiance engulf you in complete and utter luxurious value. Say to yourself, I am luxurious value. I am one of a kind. I am worthy. I honor myself and my value. I deserve it. You may also speak to your DNA and tell it to hold more light. This is what is meant by en-light-en-ment.

## ELEVATE YOUR VIBRATION

Let's calibrate your energy field to this chapter's essential intention of your ability to resonate with your desire. Here are some power phrases that align with your thoughts, feelings, actions and responses. *I know how to resonate with my desires. It's easy for me to change my resonance as a multidimensional being. I feel the resonance of my desire in my heart when I select my manifestations. When I take action in my daily life, I align my resonance in the direction of my abundance. I respond positively in my everyday circumstances because I know that I am a magical manifester worthy of receiving and I easily respond with a change in my vibrational resonance.*

### KEYS TO REMEMBER

You have lived many lifetimes with the same people. This has created a resonance field in your body which impacts what you continue to attract into your life. You had many other lifetimes and have developed other talents. You can reconnect to some of these through multiple methods. To bring something new into your life, you must learn to resonate with the new. One way to do this is to recognize your value. You are infinitely valuable. Ask yourself, "What do I want to resonate with?" Then align your energy to that desire.

# CHAPTER 6: BECOMING A PURPOSEFUL MANIFESTER

## Intention: I Am Taking Inspired Action Now.

### Invocation to Reconnect to the Greater Plan

*I let go of all that is not love*

*And embrace my Higher Self from above*

*I choose to remember the truth of who I Am*

*And Reconnect to the Greater Plan*

*That only love is real*

*My voice kisses this to seal*

Taking action in life definitely moves us in a direction, but if that action is not in alignment with our purpose or Higher Self, then we are simply going to manifest randomly or with the belief systems that are running in the background. In this chapter, I would like to explore what it means to be purposeful so that we can start to manifest a more abundant and joyful life, a life that is inspired and in harmony with the soul and the personality.

## WHAT IS PURPOSE

Most of us probably think of purpose as an activity, as something we DO in life. However, the Pleiadians have a different take on the meaning of purpose. Here is a message from the Pleiadians regarding finding purpose.

**Purpose is not an object to be found. Rather, it is a process that is part of your everyday existence.** You agree to come to Earth and serve the One. This is everyone's purpose. But how this is accomplished is through the unique individual's DNA coding, the personality and the free will choices that come up every day. It is an unfolding this process you call "purpose." It is fluid with many intersections based on those choices.

The DNA coding comes from the chosen ancestral lineage, the chosen time and place of birth, and the chosen selections made prior to incarnation. For example, two souls could have similar DNA coding, ancestors and exact time and place of birth and still have very unique experiences. For each soul carefully chooses what is going to be worked on both karmically and for soul growth and development. It is all carefully planned before coming into a body.

Knowing that you will go through the veil of amnesia brings in the fun and adventure of the Earth experience. It brings in the very temporary illusion to make it all work. Because if you remembered it at all, it would not be very easy to take seriously, would it? Your Earthly personality would not have an opportunity to grow and contribute because the greater soul would easily dominate it. As Pleiadians, we observe the whole process and bring assistance when we are invited to do so. We are not allowed to interfere with this important process. We are happy to assist when called for the aid of the soul's growth and development.

Here is another beautiful description of the human purpose path:

**The path of the human is to bloom like the flower.** Roses are not daisies, but both are beautiful. Each human is meant to bloom in their own authentic expression. A loveliness that is unique with the proper amount of nutrients, water, sunlight and soil to match. If any of these can hurt the flower, too little and she may never bloom at all. What cycle are you in and what do you need to bloom to your fullest?

Many are trapped in fixed thought patterns for these are like well-traveled roads. It's not easy to take the machete and cut through the jungle and forge a new path. This takes discipline, diligence and desire that burns in the heart for change.

## BENEFITS OF PURPOSEFUL MANIFESTING

Becoming a purposeful manifester offers numerous benefits that can bring deep fulfillment and a sense of meaning to your existence. Here are some key benefits:

1. **Sense of Direction**: Having a clear sense of purpose provides a guiding light, helping you navigate life's decisions and choices. It gives you a sense of direction, enabling you to make aligned choices that are in harmony with your values, passions, and long-term goals.

2. **Motivation and Drive:** When you have a purpose, you naturally experience a higher level of motivation and drive. Purpose ignites your inner fire, fueling your determination and perseverance to overcome challenges and pursue your goals with unwavering dedication.

3. **Enhanced Well-being and Happiness:** Living a purposeful life has been linked to increased well-being and happiness. When you're engaged in

activities that align with your purpose, you experience a sense of fulfillment, contentment, and joy. Purpose brings a deeper level of satisfaction that transcends momentary pleasures.

4. **Greater Resilience:** Purpose provides a strong foundation during difficult times. It acts as an anchor, helping you weather storms and bounce back from setbacks with resilience and optimism. Purpose fuels your inner strength and enables you to find meaning and growth even amidst adversity.

5. **Impact and Contribution:** Living a purposeful life allows you to make a meaningful impact in the world. By aligning your actions with your purpose, you can positively influence others' lives, contribute to causes that matter to you, and leave a lasting legacy that extends beyond your own existence.

6. **Increased Self-awareness and Personal Growth:** Embracing a purposeful life invites self-reflection and introspection. It encourages you to delve deep within, understand your strengths, values, and passions, and continuously evolve and grow as an individual. Purpose becomes a catalyst for personal development and self-discovery.

7. **Alignment with Authenticity:** Living with purpose enables you to align your life with your authentic self. It encourages you to embrace your unique qualities, embrace your passions, and live in alignment with your core values. This authenticity brings a sense of congruence and harmony within yourself and in your interactions with others.

8. **Enhanced Focus and Productivity:** Purpose brings clarity and focus to your endeavors. When you have a clear sense of purpose, you can prioritize your time, energy, and resources towards activities that truly matter. This focused approach enhances your productivity and helps you make significant progress in your chosen pursuits.

Ultimately, **living a purposeful life allows you to connect with your Higher Self, make a meaningful contribution, and experience a profound sense of fulfillment and well-being.** It is a deeply personal and transformative journey that enriches every aspect of your existence.

## HOW DO YOU SHOW UP FOR YOURSELF?

Sometimes we have difficulties that show up in our lives to shift us into more conscious and purposeful manifesting. Here's an example that I experienced recently. I often have potential clients sign up for an abundance discovery session with me so that I can help them explore the possibilities of what their dream life could look like. Within two weeks, I had a total of five people in a row simply not show up for their scheduled appointment. This was perplexing to me to have a pattern like this repeat so blatantly. I went into meditation and this is what my Higher Self told me:

I am helping you to complete some karmic neutralization this past month with the clients and people you know who have been absent. This is a temporary issue and is nearing completion. It is a lesson for you to show up for yourself.

How can you show up for yourself? Here is an invocation:

**I show up for myself in all ways and all dimensions.** I show up for my personal growth and spiritual evolution now and always. I show up for myself as the friend I always wanted. I show up for myself to heal any and all trauma of abandonment and let go of resistance to this healing and neutralization now. As I show up for myself, I am showing others to show up too. In truth, **I am not, nor have I ever been abandoned.** It is only when I have abandoned myself that this pattern has chosen to resurface to be healed and transformed now. I am now choosing to love and show up for myself as the Divine loves and shows up for me, which is always for eternity. Thank you and so it is.

After placing this new invocation into my heart, I began to have new clients show up again. I also gave myself permission to take some inspired action on my own behalf. I recommend setting yourself up for daily, weekly and monthly habits that anchor in more purposeful living. After all, if it's not on your calendar and in your routine, it's not in your life! Here is also a link to video I did with a singing bowl to assist you in releasing resistance: https://youtu.be/X86qbN-0FHA. I will now share with you some of my own habits for purposeful manifesting.

## SETTING NEW MOON INTENTIONS

This is a habit that I started doing after my divorce. The truth is, **if you don't track your intentions, how are you going to know what is manifesting for you or not?** The new moon represents the time of new beginnings and new life. Being in harmony with the moon and planetary cycles can assist you in being more balanced and purposeful in your own life. Here's what to do: write down 10 or 11 new intentions for the month in a journal. These are short-term goals that you want to see coming into your reality by the next new moon cycle. A funny thing started happening when I began doing this, more and more of my intentions started coming true.

The other great thing about **writing it all down is that it forces you to really think about what you want to have in your life.** For example, my husband and I wanted to sell our house in Colorado. But we were worried that it wouldn't sell right away, so we set two intentions. The first one was something like, *our house is selling easily and at our asking price.* However, we also set an intention to rent it. We wrote down, *our house is being rented to a nice family who take good care of it.* The problem with these intentions is that we created a paradox because the intention of selling was in direct conflict with renting it. After a couple of months with nothing happening, I realized my mistake and we then focused solely on selling the house.

## SETTING A DAILY INTENTION

Daily intentions can go on a sticky note or on a small white board where you can look at it throughout the day. It can align with whatever you are prioritizing for that day. Another fun thing you can do is set an alarm on your phone and put the intention as the title of the alarm so when it goes off, you are forced to read it. I often set alarms to go off at synchronistic times like 11:11, 2:22, 3:33, etc. They could even just be words of power rather than a complete sentence. Such as "smart, sexy, successful" or "inspired, abundant, purposeful." Play with word combinations and have fun with it.

## CREATING A VISION BOARD

One of My Vision Boards

They say that a picture is worth 1000 words. **A vision board is simply a way to portray your intentions in pictures.** I cut out pictures and place them on a poster board, then put the board on the wall where I can look at it regularly. You could do this once or twice per year.

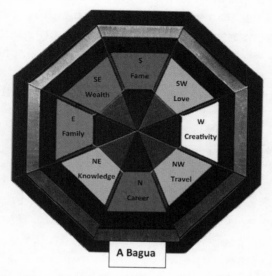

A Bagua

I've been creating vision boards for many years, organizing it with the Bagua. The Bagua is a powerful and symbolic tool used in Feng Shui, an ancient Chinese practice that seeks to harmonize and enhance the energy flow in living spaces. The Bagua, which translates to "eight areas" or "eight trigrams," is a grid-like diagram that represents different aspects of life and is overlaid onto a floor plan or space. The Bagua consists of eight sections, each corresponding to a specific area of life, such as wealth, health, relationships, career, and more. These sections are represented by various symbols, colors, and elements that embody the energetic qualities associated with each aspect.

When applied to a living or working space, the Bagua serves as a guide for arranging and optimizing the environment to promote balance, prosperity, and well-being. It helps identify areas of the space that may require attention or enhancements to support the desired intentions and goals of the occupants.

By understanding the principles of the Bagua, you can strategically place objects, colors, and elements in each corresponding area to enhance the flow of positive energy, known as "qi," and invite harmony and abundance into your life. The Bagua acts as a roadmap for creating an energetically balanced and supportive environment that aligns with your aspirations and intentions.

In essence, **the Bagua is a profound tool that helps you cultivate a harmonious relationship between your surroundings and your personal journey,** promoting a sense of well-being, prosperity, and spiritual connection.

## FULL MOON CEREMONY

At the full moon, I do another process that is also great fun and my husband and I do together. On a piece of paper, we **write down a list of things we are completing** or are already complete with.

This can include work projects, house improvement projects, negative emotions or negative experiences. Then when we both have the paper filled up, we take it to the sink and light it on fire until the paper is completely burned up. It's good to recognize what you're letting go of so that you can bring in more of the opposite.

## CREATING A CRYSTAL GRID

**An Abundance Crystal Grid**

Since moving to Sedona, I love to work with crystals. **Each one holds a specific vibration to assist us with our manifesting.** When we place them together into a grid and set an intention around the grid, we essentially create a vortex in alignment with that intention. You can create a crystal grid for just about anything. I recommend putting a clear quartz in the center, because it amplifies the effectiveness of the other crystals around it. You can also take a photograph of your grid and keep it with you or put the photo in your vision board to hold the vibration of your intention.

## FINDING PURPOSE IN FINGERPRINTS

In his book *LifePrints*, Richard Unger talked about how our **fingerprints map out our purpose.** I have been working with this system for over 15 years and my thousands of clients have found profound benefit from this system. It is truly astounding when you realize that your hands can guide you in your life purpose and I have been told over and over again from clients over the years how valuable this single piece of information is from the hands. For example, my purpose is to live my passions through the lens of wisdom. I find the most meaning in life when I am sharing what I have learned from my knowledge and experience and inspiring others through what I am most passionate about. This is one of the reasons I am driven to write.

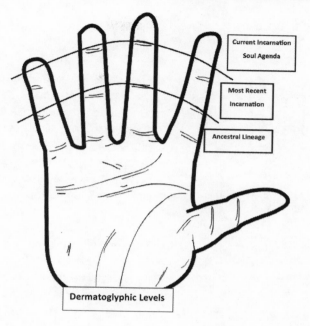

Current Incarnation
Soul Agenda

Most Recent
Incarnation

Ancestral Lineage

Dermatoglyphic Levels

**Taking fingerprints to the next level of awareness, I am learning from the Pleiadians that they are also portals into our own multidimensionality.** When you examine a finger, you will notice that you have three phalanges and there are dermatoglyphic markings across the entire palmar surface. The top level where the fingerprint is located represents the current incarnation and overall soul agenda. The middle phalange dermatoglyphics represent the most recent previous incarnation. The lower phalange dermatoglyphics represent the ancestral lineage.

Here is what the Pleiadians told me about each

## of the fingers:

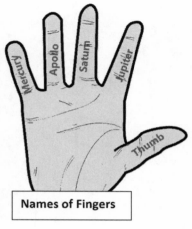

**Names of Fingers**

**The path of completion**, the right thumb, this represents the path of choosing something from one's will and following through to a sense of completion, what you also refer to as success or achievement.

**The path of power,** right Jupiter, this path is recognizing and using one's true power in one's light. To empower others this divine use of power always empowers rather than disempowers.

**The path of chosen work,** right Saturn, this is the path of experiencing a chosen profession or specific path that feels like duty. When one chooses this, it is usually chosen prior to incarnating to spend a large part of the lifetime in a specialized area of study.

**The path of creative expression,** right Apollo, this path is to be seen by others as becoming vulnerable to what others see, for all see differently when in human form. This path shows your uniqueness and how the Divine chooses to express.

**The path of the messenger,** right Mercury, this path teaches one the power of the word and the pitfalls that are common with it. One discovers the voice of divine words to embody more love and light.

**The collective path,** left thumb, one chooses not to have a personal agenda in this lifetime rather one chooses to work within the collective lessons of family lineage or ancestral clearing to be healed.

**The personal power path,** left Jupiter, this path is learning the opposite of the collective path. Choosing a lone path first even with demands of others pressing onward, not a selfish path but becomes a benefit to everyone by choosing self first. The key is knowing self versus Self and not allowing others' lower selves to interfere.

**The path of worth,** left Saturn, when one has forgotten what it means to be in harmony and integrity of the self. This comes from losing oneself to outside influences.

**The path of potential talents,** left Apollo, this path is about exploring possibilities that were left on the table with the option to pick them up again.

**The path of healing,** left Mercury, this path requires a surrender of knowingness in the intuitive realm. It requires a deep level of trust and understanding to why some things happen.

I am currently learning more and more about the fingerprints, the portals of these fingerprints and how to work with them directly from the Pleiadians. They tell me that they are teaching me processes that are part of **a branch of healing called "dermatoglyphic epigenetics."** I translate this as using finger and palmar prints to rise above one's genes. Epigenetics is a branch of biology that explores how external factors can influence gene expression without changing the underlying DNA sequence. It examines how the environment, lifestyle choices, and experiences can impact the way genes are activated or silenced, leading to changes in cellular function and potentially affecting an individual's health and well-being. Since the fingerprint pattern is a physical representation of your soul, the Pleiadians tell me that it is possible to work with these dermal ridges to direct the DNA.

Here is an example they gave me regarding the left Jupiter fingerprint.

Place the symbol for being a master manifester in your portal of left Jupiter. Here is the symbol to

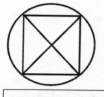

**Mastery Symbol**

use. It is useful to use when you wish to gain or claim mastery of that which you are mastering. It may also be used to work with other intentions or symbols when you are feeling deficient in an area. This helps to anchor a new level of mastery. Here is an invocation: Left Jupiter, portal open, so that I may claim my divine birthright of inner strength and self-knowledge. I choose to now anchor the full support of the universe in all dimensions my abilities to be a master manifester and see tangible results in my third dimensional realm of existence. Thank you and so it is.

They instruct me to place symbols on the fingerprint patterns and recite various invocations. If you are interested in taking this learning to a much deeper level, I offer *Portals of Ascension Mastery Certification* where you can learn more about the Pleiadian fingerprint portals, the concept of dermatoglyphic epigenetics and how to align to your highest potential. To learn more and apply, go to: https://cynthiaclark.simplero.com/page/322100.

## HOW TO KNOW YOU'RE ON PURPOSE

We are bombarded with choices every day. It's easy to become confused and think that we're somehow screwing it all up. But as we learned in the chapter about lessons, even supposed "mistakes" can be useful and purposeful. Here is advice that my Higher Self gave me:

As a co-creator of your divine pathway, you have choices to make that will affect your current and future lives. What do you wish to carry forward, for **there is no waste in creation.** When you make choices from your heart, you are working directly with the divine energy. Ask yourself why you are making a specific choice or not. And most importantly, how does it make your heart feel when the heart is at ease? The rest of the beingness of you follows. Many worthwhile endeavors are difficult, especially at the start. Look to your heart to know truth and find your focus. Ask for help and it is always available. Most of all, make choices that honor you and add to your light rather than dim it. This is the pathway of ascension.

## INDIVIDUAL VS. COLLECTIVE PURPOSE

**Because of quantum entanglement, it is easy for us to enmesh ourselves in other people's purposes and agendas.** For example, you may feel called to work with homeless people after going through a period of homelessness yourself. Life is full of choices that impact us in many ways. People who are empathic are especially vulnerable because they feel the suffering of others so deeply. It's easy for them to lose themselves in a noble cause. Here is what my guides told me about this:

Many are struggling now with the individual versus the collective. Humans embody both of these simultaneously. Each person has an individual personality and individual purpose. Yet this all affects the collective. **The best way to fulfill one's purpose is to listen to and follow the individual guidance of the Higher Self.**

This guidance cannot be heard, let alone understood or followed when one is stuck in the lower vibrations of fear, chaos and mayhem. One must come above that to hear clearly only the path of self-honoring choices that do not violate the free will of others. Then the authentic self may emerge.

Another reason not to violate free will is the creation of karma. It is important to neutralize karma through kindness to all things. When your free will is compromised, it is within your right as an equal and free being to stand up for yourself. This is called a sacred boundary. When you look at the zone of boundaries, you can see the available energy to use. We can borrow someone else's strength to assist us in many ways. This is not a violation but a way to connect to the collective. It is resistance that keeps people stuck. Think of the river and rocks in this river. Remove the rock and the raft may flow with ease. If they remove themselves from destructive forces that push fear, reconnect with themselves and then look at the choices available, this is the path forward.

This transmission referred to a part of the hands called the zone of boundaries. This is located

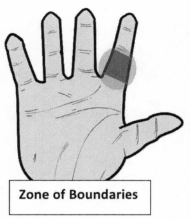

**Zone of Boundaries**

on the Jupiter finger as the lower phalange near the palm. If this zone is large relative to the rest of the other phalanges on the same finger, it shows that you have strong boundaries and a desire to be in charge. If this zone is small, then you are more easily swayed by others, and you may have a hard time standing up for yourself. You can also see blocks in this zone as horizontal lines.

**Labradorite**

I recently had a call with a potential client who was very depressed. She couldn't even see any sort of future for herself, let alone take any inspired action on her own behalf. It was interesting when one my crystals, a labradorite, fell onto my tile floor and got chipped right after I spoke with her. This particular crystal helps you with your free will. My guides told me that she was suffering from a broken free will and that there are many like her on the planet. Don't let that be you! It's time for you to take your power back.

Use this invocation:

> I choose to take back my will power and reclaim my life. I deserve peace, love and tranquility in my heart and all heart chambers.

## CALL TO ACTION

There's nothing better than setting aside time for yourself and committing to your personal growth and ascension. In my opinion, there's no better place than Sedona for this kind of transformational work and I enjoy meeting with you in person. There is a reason why Sedona is known as the spiritual capital of the United States. The vortexes here are healing, the weather is mild and there are beautiful red rocks around every corner. This is why I have set up in-person experiences in Sedona. If you're planning a vacation or are looking to experience something you can't get online, I invite you to check out https://www.sedonaspiritualdiscoveries.com for details on in-person activities.

## ELEVATE YOUR VIBRATION

Let's calibrate your energy field to this chapter's essential intention of taking inspired action. Here are some power phrases that align with your thoughts, feelings, actions and responses. *I know and recognize inspiration that leads me to take action. Taking inspired action is easy for me. Acting on my inspirations is my natural way of being. I feel inspiration in my heart when I select my manifestations. When I take action in my daily life, I follow my inspirations. I respond through my inspirations in my everyday circumstances because taking action in the moment of inspiration creates abundance, magic and miracles.*

### KEYS TO REMEMBER

Purpose is a process of your everyday existence. When you practice purposeful manifesting, it brings many benefits to you to live more fully and joyfully. Show up for yourself and the universe will show up for you. Make manifesting part of your daily, weekly, monthly and yearly routines. Fingerprints not only reveal your purpose, they are also portals into your multidimensionality. Recognize when you're under collective influence and set appropriate boundaries.

# CHAPTER 7: HANDLING TRIGGERS, SETBACKS AND DISAPPOINTMENTS

**Intention: I Continue To Respond With Knowingness And Optimism That My Desires Are Arriving In New Ways Just Right For Me.**

### Invocation for a Bright Future

*I claim my worthiness for a spectacular life.*

*I release doubt, fear, despair and strife.*

*I see the best possible outcomes coming true.*

*Love, worthiness, happiness, success sticks to me like glue.*

*I am a divine child of God.*

*My co-creation is approaching faster than a lightning rod.*

Triggers and setbacks are normal. Setbacks are a natural part of life's journey, and overcoming them requires resilience, determination, and a positive mindset. In this chapter, let's explore some effective ways to navigate and overcome setbacks.

## EMBRACE A GROWTH MINDSET

**Adopt a mindset that views setbacks as opportunities for growth and learning.** Reframe setbacks as valuable lessons and stepping stones toward success. Cultivate a belief that challenges can be overcome with effort, perseverance, and adaptation. As an entrepreneur since I was 24 years old, I've learned that sometimes even the worst setbacks can be for my benefit. I still remember when I was preparing to open my own restaurant. It took about two years of preparation and every dime of my life savings. My husband and needed a small business loan to purchase property and put up a building for it. Everything seemed like it was going well, we had all the necessary approvals and we were ready to sign the papers. Then we got a call from the bank. He said that even though everything was approved, they had just hired a new bank Vice President and he was requiring another $20,000 in collateral. Given that we were already completely maxed out, this was impossible at the time.

The loan fell through and we were unable to make the deal happen with the property we were considering. I went home and cried, feeling like the universe was so unfair. I thought that my dream was over and I would be stuck working for someone else the rest of my life. This was not the end, however. The very next day we received a phone call from the business owner who rented bicycles and who was planning on being our tenant in the building. He said that another building was already being constructed right across the street from where we were planning on opening our restaurant.

It turned out, they needed tenants and we ended up moving in there instead. It actually worked out even better than we could have imagined. We had more parking, no need for a bank loan and were a simple right turn in from the street where the traffic flowed in the afternoon when we were busiest. Two years later we ended up purchasing the property and the other business in the building, which greatly increased our value and overall bottom line. Looking back on that experience, I know now that my guides were protecting me and putting me in the best position to be successful. It didn't work out the way I had originally envisioned, it manifested even better.

## PRACTICE SELF-COMPASSION

Be kind and compassionate toward yourself when facing setbacks. Acknowledge that setbacks are part of the human experience and not a reflection of your worth or abilities. Treat yourself with understanding, patience, and self-care during challenging times. One way to energetically **practice self-love is by placing a loving bubble around yourself.**

Regarding bubbles, you may immerse yourself in other bubbles of love as you wish. For example, a bubble of self-love is highly beneficial. So you may make choices that honor you rather than keep you in low vibrations of abuse energy. Do this whenever you are feeling vulnerable or are not thinking high vibrational honoring thoughts. It will help you to keep your vibration elevated regardless of what occurs around you.

## ANALYZE AND LEARN

Take time to reflect on the setback and analyze the factors that contributed to it. Identify lessons learned and insights gained from the experience. Use this knowledge to make adjustments, develop new strategies, and avoid repeating similar mistakes in the future. It's also important to remember that **the universe returns back to you what you**

**believe to be true about your reality.** My guides call it a wave collapse – when you think of infinite possibilities existing simultaneously, but only one of those possibilities becomes your reality. As you change yourself, you change your reality. Specifically, as you change your thoughts, feelings, actions and responses, your reality reflects back the changes. Here is what they said about this:

When you talk about possibility, maybe some people don't realize the infinite timelines that collapse into a single reality, based upon the belief of the individual creating a wave collapse. **These waves collapses are shiftable as one becomes more open to change.** This is why the ability to change is so important if one wants to create a new or different reality than the one currently being experienced.

Here is an invocation to affirm while activating the lao gong point:

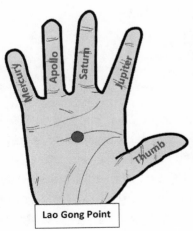

Lao Gong Point

*I am open to change. I can change. I am changing. I am safe to change I allow and welcome change.*

Apply this to your own life as you realize it is not the future that needs to change or the circumstances. It is only yourself and your perception that created the wave collapse in the first place.

The lao gong point is located at the center of the palm where the tip of the middle finger touches the palm when you make a fist.

## SET CLEAR GOALS AND PLANS

Set clear, specific goals that align with your values and aspirations. Break them down into actionable steps and create a plan to achieve them. Having a well-defined path can provide focus, direction, and a sense of purpose, making it easier to bounce back from setbacks. I'm a big fan of calendars. **Write down what you want to see manifesting in your reality.** Please refer to the previous chapter for activities and action steps you can take to support your goals and intentions.

## SEEK SUPPORT

Reach out to your support network, such as friends, family, mentors, or coaches, during challenging times. This one can be hard for some people, especially the empaths, because they tend to carry the burdens. Share your experiences and seek advice or guidance. Surrounding yourself with positive and encouraging individuals can provide emotional support, valuable insights, and different perspectives. Sometimes we may even feel like if we're too happy, then we feel guilty because so many others are not. First, we need to allow ourselves to be ok with being happy. Here is what my guides told me about this:

There is a repressed joy that is staying under the heart surface, that you are not allowing to emerge. A part of you feels like there is much suffering in the world and it wouldn't be appropriate if you embody too much joy. It is now time to let this surface again for it actually uplifts the collective joy and potential for the planet's ascension when we hold joy in our field.

Here is an invocation for you to use:

Thank you, God, for allowing me to be a catalyst for joy to be unleashed in the collective planetary field. so that I may experience a higher dimensional plane of existence, for joy is a conscious choice, just as sadness and suffering is. **I now allow joy into my field again to express fully and completely.** Thank you. And so it is.

## PRACTICE RESILIENCE

Cultivate resilience by developing coping mechanisms and stress management techniques. **Engage in activities that boost your mental and emotional well-being,** such as exercise, meditation, journaling, or engaging in hobbies you enjoy. Build your emotional strength to better navigate setbacks. Most importantly, don't forget to call on your guides in the spirit realm. One day, when I was struggling with an argument, they came to me and told me about "sparkles of positivity."

> You can push away negativity and pull to You that which you treasure. You may access sparkles of positivity. When something unpleasant is occurring, ask for the sparkles of positivity to surround the person or situation that is unpleasant. This will instantly neutralize the negative momentum and begin a polar reversal. For you live in polarity, things are constantly moving in flux towards negative or positive polarity. Try it out on all those things that seem negative to you. Once they get "blasted" with the sparkles of positivity, you will begin to see more favorable results. Go ahead and try it out today. These sparkles are high vibrations of love, joy, laughter and fun.

## FOCUS ON SOLUTIONS

Instead of dwelling on the setback itself, shift your focus toward finding solutions and taking action. Break down the problem into manageable parts and brainstorm possible solutions. **Take proactive steps toward resolving the setback and regaining momentum.**

Do not hold on to anything out of fear of lack. You are a magical manifester and have no need to worry at all. **Remember the abundance that you are and that you create around you at all times.** A good question to ask is 'am I infinitely abundant?' Does this decision make sense for me right now? Keep affirming what your soul truly is. For now it's the time to demonstrate all that you are. Know that no matter your choice, you are always honored for those choices. All choices lead to the light eventually, whether through darkness first or on the sunshine pathway. Celebrate your creations and know they are not wasted.

## MAINTAIN A POSITIVE MINDSET

Cultivate a positive attitude and belief in your ability to overcome challenges. **Use affirmations, visualization, and positive self-talk to maintain optimism and resilience.** Surround yourself with positive influences, inspiring stories, and motivational resources to stay uplifted. What you focus on expands. Long-term studies have shown that individuals with a more optimistic outlook tend to live longer. For example, a study published in the Proceedings of the National Academy of Sciences found that optimistic individuals had a significantly lower risk of mortality over a follow-up period of 30 years. Optimistic people often engage in healthier behaviors, which can contribute to their longevity. They are more likely to engage in regular exercise, maintain a balanced diet, practice stress management techniques, and adhere to medical treatments when necessary.

Optimistic individuals tend to cope with stress more effectively, which can have a positive impact on their overall health. They may have stronger social support networks, engage in problem-solving strategies, and exhibit higher levels of resilience, all of which contribute to better health outcomes. **Optimism has been linked to a lower risk of developing various chronic conditions,** such as cardiovascular disease, hypertension, and depression. Optimistic individuals may have lower levels of inflammation, healthier cardiovascular profiles, and a stronger immune system, which can contribute to better overall health and longevity. Optimism is associated with improved mental health and well-being. Positive emotions and a resilient mindset can buffer against the negative effects of stress, reduce the risk of mental health disorders, and contribute to a higher quality of life.

## PRACTICE ADAPTABILITY

Be open to adapting your plans and strategies as circumstances change. **Be flexible and willing to explore alternative routes to your goals.** Embrace change as an opportunity for growth and evolution rather than resisting it. The Arcturians came in during one of my meditations and offered a procedure to assist you in shifting emotional debris. It's so easy

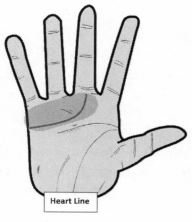

Heart Line

to get caught up in emotional flare-ups as things change around you. I certainly know that I can get angry sometimes when things don't go the way I want them to! The Arcturians shared a process to do with the heart line in the hands. The heart line is a major line located just under the

fingers. Like all lines, reading the heart line is complicated. Essentially, **the heart line reveals how you feel and how much you feel.** It also shows how you express those feelings or not. The first picture shows where

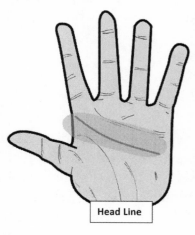

Head Line

the heart line is located. The head line is similar to the heart line and runs roughly horizontally through the middle part of the palm. **It reveals how you think and how much you think.** For the purposes of this exercise, it is not important for you to read these lines so much as it is just to know where

they are on your hands. Take a moment to locate your

heart line and head line. They will be on both hands.

We are here to share with you a process to elevate your emotions to a new level that works with the heart line. You may run your nail or a crystal point over your heart line, first with the releasing of the undesired emotion, such as inadequacy or not good enough or unsupported. Say "I release (emotion) in all dimensions from all heart chambers now." Go ahead and try it for yourself. Then go over the line again with your new desired emotion. Say "I am feeling completely (desired emotion) in all dimensions and in all heart chambers now." As you repeat this on both hands, you will feel a shift in your energy. **This process is good to quickly shift the emotional debris that may be hindering you from achieving higher states of love and bliss,** making your manifesting easier. The same process may be applied to the head line for repetitive thoughts that are clogging up an otherwise efficient manifestation. Your lines are like pipes, as a type of plumbing for your emotions and thoughts to be delivered.

## KEEP MOVING FORWARD

Even in the face of setbacks, maintain forward momentum. **Take consistent action, however small, toward your goals.** You may have heard that when you take one step toward your goal, the universe takes ten towards you. Therefore, if you take one step per day for a year, you will have taken 365 steps in one year and the universe will have taken 3,650! Now that's progress! **Celebrate small victories and milestones** along the way to maintain motivation and a sense of progress.

My guides have spoken to me about divine time. This is another way to keep moving forward.

> Speak love and enter divine time. Divine time is being in flow with how and not when something comes into alignment for you. D.I.V.I.N.E. stands for divine interception victorious in nebulous environment. How to know if you're in divine time? 1. You see synchronicities; 2. You feel time speed up or slow down; 3. Things or people that used to matter don't anymore; 4. You seek spiritual truth; 5. Things or people show up when you need them.

A nebulous environment represents the birthplace of stars, so this means that a divine environment shows you where to birth your dreams and goals. Synchronicities happen to me all the time. Let's first talk about what a synchronicity is. Synchronicity is a concept introduced by Swiss psychologist Carl Jung to describe meaningful coincidences that seem to occur outside the realm of conventional cause-and-effect relationships. It refers to the occurrence of two or more events that are meaningfully related, even though they may not have a direct causal connection.

In synchronistic experiences, events or situations align in a way that feels significant or meaningful to the individual involved. These events often appear to be highly improbable or unlikely, yet they carry a sense of purpose, connection, or a deeper underlying message. Here are some examples.

Synchronicities are subjective experiences and can vary in their nature and significance for different individuals. They can manifest in various forms, such as:

1. **Symbolic Coincidences:** Synchronicities often involve symbols, themes, or patterns that hold personal meaning to the individual. For example, coming across a specific animal or repeatedly encountering certain numbers or phrases that hold significance to the person.

2. **Timely Encounters:** Synchronistic experiences may involve chance meetings or encounters with people who bring valuable insights, guidance, or opportunities at the right moment. These encounters can lead to transformative experiences or a shift in life's direction.

3. **Serendipitous Events:** Synchronicities can manifest as unexpected events or occurrences that seem to align perfectly with a person's needs, desires, or intentions. It may involve finding a solution to a problem just when it's needed, stumbling upon resources or information that were sought after, or experiencing a series of events that lead to a desired outcome.

4. **Intuitive Guidance:** Synchronicities can serve as a form of intuitive guidance, offering subtle messages or nudges from the universe or a higher power. They may provide reassurance, affirmation, or insights into one's life path, decisions, or spiritual growth.

**Synchronicities are often interpreted as indications of a deeper interconnectedness between the individual and the universe.** They suggest that there may be an underlying order or pattern to life that extends beyond conventional explanations. Many people see synchronicities as a confirmation of being on the right path, a reminder of the interconnectedness of all things, or a sign of spiritual significance. It's important to note that synchronicities are subjective experiences and can be interpreted in various ways based on personal beliefs and perspectives. They can hold personal meaning and significance to individuals, providing a sense of wonder, inspiration, and a feeling of being part of something greater than oneself.

Before I founded Ascension17.com, I started seeing the number 717 or variations of it multiple times per day. At first, I had no idea what it meant or what it wanted me to know. Only after speaking with my Higher Self did I learn that the 7 represented my own spiritual path and the 17 was representing the number of ascension and the progression of Earth and Earth's inhabitants into the next stage of spiritual growth.

One of My Synchronicities

To this day, I still see this number quite often. For example, when I was first deciding whether or not to learn how to fly an airplane, I thought about it for about a month. When I eventually found North Aire Aviation, I learned that it was 71.7 miles away from my home in Sedona. They had a Cessna 172 that was in their fleet and it had the tail number N17304 (3 + 0 + 4 = 7.) I often arrive or depart from my home at 7:17. Or I will notice the temperature outside is 71 degrees and the humidity is 17 percent. I saw a license plate the other day with 7771111. These things are common occurrences for me. The universe loves to communicate through numbers and number patterns. What numbers do you see?

## ELEVATE YOUR VIBRATION

Let's calibrate your energy field to this chapter's essential intention of your ability to respond with knowingness and optimism. Here are some power phrases that align with your thoughts, feelings, actions and responses. *I know how to stay optimistic as I wait for my desires to manifest. Optimism is easy for me. Being optimistic is my natural way of being. I feel optimism in my heart when I select my manifestations. When I take action in my daily life, I am optimistic that I am moving in the direction of my abundance. I respond with knowingness and optimism in my everyday circumstances because I trust and resonate with my desires, and I know I am worthy to receive them.*

### KEYS TO REMEMBER

Setbacks are temporary challenges that offer opportunities for growth and resilience. By embracing setbacks as part of the journey and employing the various strategies described, you can overcome obstacles, learn valuable lessons, and ultimately manifest your goals.

# CHAPTER 8: LOVE ALWAYS SURROUNDS YOU

## Intention: I Am Grateful That I Am Now Attracting More And More Of My Desires.

### Invocation to Connect to the Cosmic Heart

*Cosmic Heart, I ask you to open and welcome me in*

*Thank you for your loving embrace,
always there, you are kin*

*Through you may I find my way*

*Light shine through me, here to stay*

## WE LIVE IN A BENEVOLENT UNIVERSE

Although it sometimes seems to the contrary,

we do actually live in a benevolent universe. **We have a Creator who loves us infinitely.** We are sparks of divine creation living individual experiences to bring back to the Creator when each lifetime completes. This greater love, the love of our one infinite Creator, my guides refer to as the Cosmic Heart or the Cosmic Heart Consciousness.

The Pleiadians and my other guides have been telling me throughout their transmissions that **connection to the Cosmic Heart is an important component to manifesting.** Here is a combination of transmissions that talk about the Cosmic Heart:

The Cosmic Heart is the one heart, the one love. The one light of all that is, it can be felt by anyone who chooses to connect in sincerity. It can be felt through the palms. Soon the light will vibrate through all beings and the truth will be seen by more and more. All will see the light eventually. This is the way of ascension.

When one is truly connected to the Cosmic Heart, there is no problem with creation. It is far easier to co-create and make progress in alignment with your potential. Your heart is the realm of creation. **When you bring in the Cosmic Heart, you cannot fail.** Feel it pulsing through your own precious heart.

The center of the palm is the access point to the Cosmic Heart. It is the realm of change in the body. When you place the center of your palms over your own heart, you are aligning with this infinite heart energy.

## SEPARATION IS AN ILLUSION

When we consider that we are only experiencing a small part of our reality and start to look at the bigger picture of how we are multidimensional, we begin to understand that **we are part of everything and everything is part of us.** The Pleiadian Council of Light taught us this:

Example of a Fractal

We are part of you and you are part of us. A hologram, a whole contained in the part, a pathway of divine energy to be expressed as an "individual." This is a challenging concept to understand, this is why we show you the image of the fractal, a repeating pattern that gets smaller and smaller for all eternity. **You are a part of this pattern. You are part of the weaving of the cosmic tapestry of divine light.** The choices you make on Earth radiate out of this pattern to impact the entire universe. We would like you to understand the importance you all have and the power to reverberate love into the field. For now is a time of renewal, a time of rebirth and time of remembrance. It is time for you to remember the truth of your nature, your divine nature. It is time to drop the false identities of smallness, insignificance, helplessness. The time is now to remember your placement in the cosmic pattern of All That Is.

When we begin to look at our waking lives like a dream landscape, like this holographic reality, things become more interesting. For example, if you have a leaky pipe in your house, you should ask yourself, *What emotions am I not allowing myself to express?* Anything to do with water relates to your emotions. Or perhaps you have a boss who doesn't appreciate you. What underlying self-worth needs to be claimed within yourself? When I had vertigo shortly after my divorce to my first husband, the illness was showing me that I felt like my life was out of control. If you see lots of 555's showing up, you can recognize that massive changes are happening in your life. The universe is always teaching you and showing you what is going on internally. And I can guarantee that if it's showing up in your hands, it will be showing up in your life. For example, if you have a stress line in one of your fingers, it will correspond to the stress that's in your life. Change the stress and the line will disappear. Or have you ever noticed that when your house is cluttered, your life is also cluttered? One of the best things you can do is to clean and tidy your space.

## BENEFITS OF GRATITUDE

Love and gratitude are not new concepts in any spiritual practice. You probably already know that when you are grateful, your energy increases, your vibration rises, and the door opens for more and more to be grateful for. Energetically, **gratitude is a powerful and transformative state of being that can have profound effects on our overall well-being and the energy we emit.** When we are genuinely grateful, several energetic shifts occur:

1. **Positive Vibrations:** Gratitude emits positive and high-frequency vibrations. It elevates our energy field and aligns us with feelings of joy, abundance, and contentment. These positive vibrations can influence our surroundings and attract similar positive energies and experiences.

2. **Expanded Awareness:** Gratitude opens us up to the present moment and expands our awareness. It shifts our focus from what may be lacking or challenging to what we appreciate and value in our lives. This expanded awareness allows us to see the beauty, blessings, and opportunities that surround us.

3. **Heart Coherence:** Gratitude activates the heart

center, promoting coherence and harmonious energy within our body-mind system. When we feel genuine gratitude, our heart rhythm becomes more coherent, creating a positive influence on our overall well-being and radiating a harmonious energy outward.

4. **Shift in Perspective:** Gratitude helps shift our perspective from a mindset of lack or negativity to one of abundance and positivity. It reframes our experiences, challenges, and circumstances, allowing us to see the lessons, growth, and blessings within them. This shift in perspective can bring about a sense of peace, acceptance, and empowerment.

5. **Attraction of Abundance:** Gratitude aligns us with the energy of abundance. By focusing on what we are grateful for, we cultivate an attitude of abundance and sufficiency. This energetic alignment can attract more positive experiences, opportunities, and blessings into our lives.

6. **Improved Relationships:** Expressing gratitude fosters positive connections and deeper relationships with others. When we genuinely appreciate and acknowledge others, we create a ripple effect of positivity, strengthening the energetic bonds between individuals and enhancing the overall energy of the relationships.

7. **Emotional Balance:** Gratitude helps regulate our emotions and promotes emotional well-being. It can uplift our mood, reduce stress, anxiety, and depression, and increase feelings of happiness and contentment. This emotional balance contributes to a more harmonious and balanced energy field.

8. **Alignment with Higher Self:** Gratitude connects us to our Higher Self or spiritual essence. It cultivates a sense of connection, trust, and surrender to the greater forces at play in the universe. This alignment with our Higher Self allows us to tap into intuitive guidance, wisdom, and a deeper understanding of our purpose and interconnectedness.

Overall, gratitude has a transformative effect on our energetic state. It raises our vibrations, expands our awareness, and aligns us with positive energies and experiences. By practicing gratitude regularly, we can cultivate a more harmonious, abundant, and joyful energy that influences all aspects of our lives.

**LOVE AND ASCENSION**

This concept of love, Christ Consciousness, the rapture, ascension, all these things involve us being able to hold more and more of this higher love within ourselves so that we may move into our next dimensional reality. Here is what the Pleiadian Council of Light had to share about it:

> We are here to communicate with you tonight and share valuable insights that you may choose to share with those who have ears to hear us. We are wanting to share the message for you today that your ascension process is assured for your planet and **you are moving toward the next dimensional experience very soon.** The step that is MOST important right now at this delicate juncture is to accept and **access higher states of love and bliss.** When more and more of you on the planet practice this, it creates an acceleration effect for those who are stubbornly holding on to the lower vibrations of fear, chaos, worry, etcetera. **The best way to remember love is to remind yourself that you came from love, you are love and you are here to spread love.** For that is what the Divine is, what the One is made of. Spreading infinite love and bliss. This is the soul's pathway through chosen individual entities. Claim your divine love now and feel it move across your planet in a soft pink wave of energy. Let it penetrate every cell in your own body and heal all wounds that are ready to heal, for not all wounds are ready. Sometimes there is a progression in healing. It is whatever is appropriate for the soul.

Here's an invocation for you to unite your own mind and heart with the Cosmic Heart. Say this invocation with the center of your palms placed over your heart.

*I choose to unite my mind and heart with the Cosmic Heart to fulfill my highest potential and purpose that was chosen for me, and that I chose prior to incarnating in this lifetime. I welcome and allow my freewill to align with my Higher Self and Source energy to guide my daily thoughts, feelings, actions and reactions in my best and highest good as well as the best and highest good of those I am in connection with. Thank you and so it is.*

## THE VIOLET FLAME

The concept of the Violet Flame is associated with the spiritual teachings and belief systems of various esoteric and metaphysical traditions. It is often attributed to the Ascended Master St. Germain, a spiritual figure believed to have lived in different incarnations and achieved spiritual enlightenment. I have worked with the Violet Flame over the years and recently had St. Germaine and Archangel Uriel come to me with a meditation, which I share below.

**The Violet Flame is described as a high-frequency, transformative energy that is said to possess powerful cleansing and purifying qualities.** It is envisioned as a spiritual flame or energy that has the ability to transmute negative energies, thoughts, emotions, and karmic patterns into positive, harmonious vibrations.

Key aspects and beliefs related to the Violet Flame include:

1. **Transmutation:** The Violet Flame is believed to have the power to transform and transmute lower vibrational energies into higher frequencies. It is seen as a catalyst for spiritual growth, healing, and personal transformation.

2. **Cleansing and Purification:** The Violet Flame is associated with purifying and cleansing the aura, energy field, and subtle bodies of individuals. It is believed to help release and dissolve negative karma, emotional blockages, and energetic imbalances.

3. **Spiritual Protection:** The Violet Flame is also seen as a form of spiritual protection. By invoking and working with the Violet Flame, individuals aim to create a protective energetic shield around themselves, preventing the influence of negative energies or entities.

4. **Divine Love and Forgiveness:** The Violet Flame is often connected with the qualities of divine love and forgiveness. It is believed to help individuals release and heal deep-seated emotional wounds, promote forgiveness of oneself and others, and foster a sense of compassion and unconditional love.

5. **Spiritual Ascension:** The Violet Flame is associated with the spiritual path of ascension, raising consciousness and vibrational frequency to higher levels of spiritual awareness and connection. It is viewed as a tool for accelerating spiritual growth and evolution.

The Violet Flame is like the water in the shower, purifying and cleansing everything. Let your imagination see rain as Violet Flames and cleanse everything before placing it in your heart. See the Violet Flame rain falling on your body. It is a cool and refreshing flame of divine light. Allow the Violet Flame first into the heart. Then let it move up to the eyes and the third eye and finally the Crown while letting the crystal purpurite anchor where it is most useful. Place the Violet Flame inside your heart. Let it burn forever in your energy field. Feel the Violet Flame now as it cleanses and purifies all remaining doubt you may still hold from your not-self. Take helpless, drop the "less," which leaves help. H.E.L.P. I am honored, enlightened, loved and protected. This is what remains.

## LOVE INTERVENTIONS

Have you ever had any magical or mystical experiences that happen to you in your life? I would love to share a couple of stories with you now so that you may realize that the Divine Creator is always there, ever knowing, and comes to you when you are in need.

## THE PINK BUBBLE

It was October in the Camelback mountains just outside of Scottsdale, Arizona. My husband and I were hiking up to a place called Tom's Thumb. This hike was pretty much in the sun the entire way. It was a classic dry desert landscape with mostly cacti, but not very many trees. We left the parking lot around 10:00 in the morning, and we thought we could be back within about three hours, coming back around 1:00 in the afternoon. I realized after about 30 minutes of hiking that **I had forgotten to put on my sunscreen.** This was when I began to panic because I have very fair skin and I typically burn very easily and quickly under the hot Arizona sun.

Even though it was October, I knew it was going to get up to close to 100 degrees by the time we were finished. I was only wearing shorts and a tank top. My shoulders were exposed. My legs were exposed. Part of my upper chest was exposed. At least I was wearing a hat and sunglasses so my face had a little bit of protection. What I did know were two things. First, it was too late to turn back and second, I was wondering how badly my skin going to burn. There were no other hikers around, either, so I couldn't ask anyone if they had sunscreen to spare.

Just as this panic and realizations were happening, I suddenly heard a voice come into my head. **The voice told me to place a pink bubble around me for protection against the sun.** It said to call it in and ask it to protect me. This was a peculiar thought because I had never heard of this pink bubble before and I certainly would never have thought of that on my own. Rather than question it, I immediately followed the advice of this voice. I called in the energy of a pink bubble to surround me and my husband and to protect both of us from any damaging rays that the sun might burn our skin.

We ended up doing our hike as planned. By the

time we got down, it was close to the 1 pm timeline that we had anticipated. Normally my pale skin would be like a cooked lobster at this point, and it was very hot. But to my surprise and delight I did not have a single burn on me, nor did my husband!

I began to develop a new relationship with this pink bubble and have tested it out many times since this hike. Now this is my new sunscreen. **I don't actually use sunscreen anymore.** I just call in the pink bubble of protection anytime that I go outside, especially if it's going to be a hot, summery day. And I don't worry about getting burned anymore.

This is a great example of being in your mojo. I use my intentions and knowingness for so much. For example, whenever I am driving somewhere crowded, I call in my parking angels and I always get a good parking space. Whenever I go somewhere that others might consider shady or questionable, I call in my protectors. I envision the best possible outcome and have a deep sense of faith in the divine working with me.

**ANGELS IN HUMAN FORM**

I was recently travelling again to Scottsdale, which is my favorite part of Phoenix. We had gone down for my husband to get eye surgery and I was the designated driver. We were just about to return our rental car, a black Kia, back to the airport. I needed to top off the tank before heading out. I find this incredibly funny, in that I can fly a small airplane, my Cessna 182, but sometimes I can't even open a gas cap, especially if it's in a car I've never driven before. I'm used to my BMW where all I need to do is push on the cover and it opens up. This Kia had some sort of lock on it and I couldn't figure it out. My husband, who just had his surgery, was not going to be able to help either.

Within just a few seconds, this very nice young man came over to assist me. I didn't even tell him what was wrong. He was about 5'10" tall, slim and had a well-trimmed beard that was somewhat reddish in color. He came right over to the car and pointed to the side of the driver's seat. He said, "I think this is where you can open it up." Sure enough, that was exactly right and I got the cover open so we could fill the tank. I turned around to thank the young man for his help, but he had completely disappeared! Even my husband said that he didn't know where he came from or where he went to. I'm convinced that he was an angel.

I've had various encounters over the years that I now believe were angelic encounters. They seemed to arrive out of nowhere and show up when I really needed to hear something comforting. They were always so positive and direct, as if they knew me and what was in my heart. And they also left just as quickly.

## LOVE IS THE ANSWER

**The guides continue to affirm that love is the answer to everything.** To manifest anything in your life, you simply can't do it from a place of anger, hatred, judgment, sadness, denial or any of the lower vibrational emotional states. When I do group manifesting with my clients, I tell them how important it is to be in a positive state of mind and heart before coming to the session. I know this is challenging when we are bombarded with so much negativity all the time, that's why it is so important to discipline yourself and create new habits.

Here's one that came through in a meditation:

**Focus on love and being loving as much as possible even and especially with those who are demonstrating not-love.** This is a hard task we know but can be achieved with discipline. Breathe love into your body. This is the connection you have with the divine. It is a balancer, one must have the inhalation and the exhalation process. Count all the things you are grateful for. The more you are in gratitude, the more in alignment with love and the negative shall dissipate. Speak words of love and support first and foremost to yourself, then to those around you when you hear not-love. Speaking not-love halts your vibrational advancement. This is a simple reminder of your power. You are a powerful co-creator.

Use these words of power: Love is here, I breathe in love, I am grateful for the love I have and I share love with you now. This process resets your pineal gland in your body so that you may hold more light in order to raise your vibration ever so gently.

## Here's another one:

The veil of amnesia is lifting for those who have already balanced with their karma. For those still working, it is coming, and the veil will continue to thin out. Remember your magnificence and the power you have always had but had forgotten. This is the power to create change, to fuse love together as the diamond is created and transformed from what it once was. **Grasp the energy of love for love is the true source of power. It is love that dissolves the lower vibrational energy.** Love is the key. Hold love in your vibrational field so that it may affect those around you.

Here is an invocation to place in your heart:

I release all that is not-love to be transformed to love. I choose to hold and embody love in my heart. Let love light my path and all that surrounds me. Thank you and so it is.

## THERE IS NO LIMIT TO YOUR POTENTIAL

If you knew that you had no limits to what you could create, what would you choose? The guides tell me so often how powerful we are, if only we knew how much. As you connect to and recognize your multidimensionality, you begin to understand the truth of this. I encourage you to question your so-called reality, because I know that it can change. **By anchoring in the eight essential intentions, your life is going to look a lot different in a short amount of time.**

There is no limit to your potential. All beings are pure potential. Limits only happen as we collapse a belief in a possibility, this is why it is important to keep believing in what is possible because all things are possible.

I would like to challenge you to start thinking

bigger, about yourself AND what's possible for you. **A question that I like to ask myself is, what else is possible?** What more is possible? What do I really want? Now is the time to take charge of your life and become a multidimensional manifester! One of my programs, called *Spiritual Abundance Mastery*, assists you in mastering the Law of Attraction, entering the realm of creation and giving you the opportunity to practice group manifesting, where all the members uplift each other's intentions. If you would like to check out some free training to get started, you may access it with this link: https://cynthiaclark.simplero.com/page/271155.

## ACCESSING HIGHER TRUTH

The Ascended Masters wanted me to leave you with this invocation to move forward in your own spiritual growth and divine pathway.

We are here to assist you and those who are ready to learn about the nature of your reality so that you may progress in your soul evolution. For this was a path you chose to embark on. The higher truth remains hidden until it is divine time to know and use the wisdom we have accumulated in a time beyond time.

When you are ready for your crystal-clear knowingness to present to you, here is an invocation:

**I choose to access my divine birthright of higher truth and express it in a way that is in alignment with my soul's agenda and highest potential.** May I see clearly and without fear or doubt all that I may benefit from knowing so that my vibration matches this higher truth and recognizes it as truth rather than something I question or forget. For forgetfulness is sometimes appropriate, but I now claim my readiness to remember. May I only use this higher truth as a way to ascend and assist others to ascend for that is the path of the One, that was co-created in the realm of Creation. May I flow with ease, love, joy and gratitude as I am able to comprehend more and more with ease and divine clarity. Thank you and so it is.

This invocation shall open the door to receive spontaneous higher truth as you need it. It will flow with ease and grace into your divine path. We look forward to sharing truth with you.

## ELEVATE YOUR VIBRATION

Let's calibrate your energy field to this chapter's essential intention of being grateful that you are now attracting more and more of your desires. Here are some power phrases that align with your thoughts, feelings, actions and responses. *I know how to be grateful. Gratitude is easy for me. Gratitude is my natural way of being. I feel gratitude in my heart when I select my manifestations. When I take action in my daily life, I remain grateful that I am moving in the direction of my abundance. I respond with gratitude in my everyday circumstances because I know that I am now attracting more and more of my desires.*

## KEYS TO REMEMBER

We live in a benevolent universe and it IS possible to create the life of your dreams. Separation from the Divine Creator is a temporary but convincing illusion. Practicing gratitude opens the door for more abundance to flow into our lives. Moving into higher states of love and bliss is the answer to everything. It is possible to see love and divine interventions on a regular basis. Cultivate knowingness in your unlimited potential to manifest a more abundant life.

# EPILOGUE

I hope that you now feel empowered to move forward not only in your mojo of manifesting, but also in your spiritual ascension. The Arcturians wanted me to share a message regarding being multidimensional. Here is what they said:

**We wish for you to claim your full abilities of ascension. To know you are able to operate outside of time-space is part of this.** We recommend that you continue to build your relationship with timelessness just as you do with agelessness. This will help you to perceive your multidimensionality with greater ease.

Say this invocation:

I am claiming my divine birthright of multidimensionality as an infinite being of Light. I recognize now that time-space is a construct of third dimensional existence, but this is only appearing as my current reality when it is not my actual reality. **I now choose to recognize my new relationship with timelessness** to be enhanced, anchored and absorbed in my energy field so that I may move more easily and freely into the next stage of my ascension mastery. For it is important to realize this concept as part of my learning. Use this symbol to anchor this concept into your energy field:

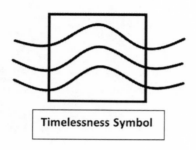

Timelessness Symbol

Place this symbol in your portal of change (the center part of your palm, the lao gong point) to create and anchor timelessness into your consciousness. As this becomes stabilized, you will begin to shift your focus away from the "past" and the "future" and know that everything exists here and now. Why is this important? **It is important to know for your manifesting to become more instantaneous; however this is only after one becomes disciplined in the workings of one's true power.** So there is a progression that is granted by the Cosmic Heart to be appropriate for each individual entity.

Clearly, with this transmission, we are moving into an amazing "time" in our spiritual development. I have personally been able to "speed up" and "slow down" time on numerous occasions, sometimes during a great need and other times simply when I needed to connect with another soul. I continue to fly my Cessna 182 as my guides have instructed, for it connects me with my multidimensional self. One day when I was flying, I snapped a picture of the glass panel and the image that

Spiritual Eye

came up was clearly a spiritual eye. They send me rainbow images quite frequently before flights, which I lovingly refer to now as the "rainbow runway." I have also witnessed several miracles with clients over the years. Here is one their stories, this coming from Sheila Tye:

"I have learned to recognize when I'm entering into magic time. This is a term I use to describe, a time when the Universe gently and lovingly relays a message through what would only be described as magic. As we grow spiritually, we deepen our connection with the Divine One, we deepen our understanding of how the universe works. Here's my story of when the moon came a knockin' on my windowpane one summer night:

I had been asleep for a few hours when I was awakened by the bright gleam from the Buck Moon, known more commonly as the Supermoon. The gleam danced upon my closed eyelids and said, wake up and come to the window. I reached up for my cell phone to see what time it was. It was then I realized I was in magic time. The time displayed on the iPhone rolled over to 2:52 a.m., and there was a hint of magic dust in the number. I immediately added these numbers, two plus five plus two together and got the number nine, which is a powerful number from the spiritual realm representing completion or fulfillment of one cycle, so you can prepare for the next one. *Come to the window.* The moon, my entire team of Angels, Spirit Guides, Ascended Masters, the Hathors, and the Pleiadian Council of Light, they all sat and beckoned.

I went to the window and raised the blinds and looked into the face of the magnificent moon. The moon was smiling as it explained to me it was waiting for my order as I did not submit any intentions, nor did I submit anything I was complete with, and it was waiting. I then said to the moon, I know you know my intentions and completions better than I. And then I heard, *you are not small nor insignificant. Step into your power. Step into your power now.* I replied, yes, I accept your request of myself. The moon said, *announce what you are complete with.* For which I replied, I am complete with feeling small and insignificant. I then went to the room where my crystals are placed, and I opened that blind and said to the moon, I trust you will fully recharge these as I sleep, and then went back to my room and told the moon I must rest now, but I will leave my blinds open so that I can rest and bathe in the moon, bathe in your ray. Also, I added a request for healing as I had not been feeling well over the past two weeks, the moon assured me, *and so it is.*

I awoke that morning refreshed and I knew I had experienced divine magic time through the night. I am learning what true love and true divine time is. It arrives for each of us when we are ready to receive and step into it. I am learning the universe supports us fully and we have an entire assigned team to assist us as we continue our journey through time. Life is forever evolving. And as humans we are blessed and evolving in our short time here on Earth. We are all loved."

## AN INVITATION AND SPECIAL OFFER

The concepts presented in this book have been instrumental in guiding you toward alignment with your purpose and ascension. However, **the path to ascension is a journey that goes beyond**

Portals of Ascension Mastery

**understanding these concepts; it requires regular spiritual practice and dedication.** If you consider yourself a spiritual high achiever, someone poised to step into your multidimensional self, embrace your highest potential, find profound purpose, and design a life you genuinely love while making a more significant impact on our world, then this program is designed just for you. Join me for an extensive offering designed especially for spiritual professionals, high achievers, and those who've delved into the pages of this book. Together, we'll dive into the wisdom of the Pleiadian Council of Light and explore the 11 hand portals, unlocking and activating them to help you align with your ultimate potential.

**Some of the benefits of this training include:**

1.  A much greater **sense of peace,** knowing that you are not, nor will you ever be alone.

2.  **Heightened abilities** and renewed awareness in those divine gifts that are your birthright, encoded in your DNA.

3.  **Renewed sovereignty** – a knowingness that no one and nothing can take away who and what you are, a divine multidimensional being whose soul is eternal.

4. **Clarity in your path, purpose, mission, direction,** being aware of your importance and how your efforts impact the Earth and the Collective Unconscious.

5. **Find joy, fun and play** as you re-connect to the part of you that knows this is all a construct and not real, but a holographic reflection that you co-created.

6. **Tools to guide you in manifesting a new Earth,** a new dawn, a new joyful exuberance that shall become your "new normal," not born from fear, but born from love and eternal connectedness to the One Infinite Creator, making it very easy to see through the current planetary illusions.

**When you master the portals of Ascension, you will:**

- Expand your infinite knowingness as a divine being

- Trust in yourself, creating more strength and courage

- Be confident in your gifts and sharing them with the world

- Feel more freedom, time for yourself and your important relationships

- Spend the majority of your time on your priorities to give you a sense of meaning and fulfillment

- Know the power of supportive boundaries that are good for everyone

- Live with more happiness and moments of joy
- Neutralize karma

- Experience increased creativity and productivity which creates more time for YOU

- Have more energy

- Increase your income, coming from an abundant vibration

- Easily stand in your power

- Work directly with your spiritual team and increase your intuition

- Courageously set boundaries that stick

- Bring in supportive and loving personal relationships

- Gather your spiritual tribe

- Attract the right collaborative and supportive people

- Heal the blocks that are ready to be released

The Pleiadians said this about the Portals of Ascension Mastery:

> We are happy to assist those who are ready and willing to explore what it means to be a multidimensional being on the path of ascension. For the brave spiritual adventurers and high achievers, this path shall take them through not only connecting to the angels and groups like us, who are part of a greater universal family, but shall **carry them through a soul discovery of deep healing and exploration of their eternal selves.** We shall be reconnecting to the Cosmic Heart not only in third density, but also in fifth density and beyond. It shall be a galactic anchoring that propels them at an accelerated rate to the next stage of their soul evolution. We shall hold their hands throughout this program, and they will learn how to clearly communicate not only with us, but other galactic beings. **Our processes shall help them to expand** – expand not only in consciousness, but in love and being able to hold higher and higher vibratory set-points for longer periods.

If you're ready to explore "dermatoglyphic epigenetics" and practice ascension principles, with me at your side, please click on this link to apply: https://cynthiaclark.simplero.com/page/322100.

For more information about ascension and spiritual abundance, you may also visit https://Ascension17.com. If you would like to learn more about my palmistry and tarot training and the Palmistry Tarot card deck, please visit www.PalmistryTarot.com. Coming to Sedona, Arizona? Check out my in-person experiences at https://www.SedonaSpiritualDiscoveries.com. And lastly, here are my social links, https://linktr.ee/ascension17.

Above all, dear reader, I wish you infinite abundance as you progress in your spiritual ascension.

# BIBLIOGRAPHY

Farrow, Mary. "Why Christians believe in resurrection, not reincarnation."

Catholic News Agency, April 12, 2020. https://www.catholicnewsagency.com/news/39710/why-christians-believe-in-resurrection-not-reincarnation

University of Bristol Department of Religion and Theology. "Death and Dying in Buddhism." Accessed March 17, 2023, http://www.bristol.ac.uk/religion/buddhist-centre/projects/bdr/chaplains/online-guide.html

Sci News. "Study: Optimism is Important Psychosocial Resource for Extending Life Span in Older Adults." August 28, 2019, https://www.sci.news/medicine/optimism-longevity-07536.html

Jones, Walter. "ALL Starseed Types: Their Secrets, Traits & Missions." Psychic Blaze, February 12, 2023. https://psychicblaze.com/starseed-types/

Kirsten, Charlotte. "25 Starseed Types: Which Star

System is Your Soul Really From?" Typically Topical, May 20, 2021. https://typicallytopical.com/starseed-types/

Brunton, Susan. "The Hathors: Venusian Starseed and Their Traits." Spiritual Unite. Accessed March 12, 2023. https://www.spiritualunite.com/articles/hathor-or-venusian-starseed-and-their-traits/

Inner Space. "The Hathors, 6-10-19. https://www.innerspeacevoyages.com/blog/the-hathors

# ABOUT THE AUTHOR

## Cynthia Clark

Cynthia has worked with over 7,000 people in the last 15 years to manifest all types of abundance. She meditates daily and channels messages from her spirit guides, Higher Self, the angelic and galactic realms. Her other works include Stories in Your Hands, Palmistry Tarot, and Palmistry Inspiration Cards. She uses her gifts in hand analysis, channeling, dermatoglyphic epigenetics and alternative healing to help others transform their lives and ascend spiritually. An entrepreneur since she was 24, a déjà-vu experience led her to study palmistry after selling her restaurant. Her multidimensional training programs not only help people manifest more abundance, but also teach ascension techniques to assist them in raising their awareness and vibration toward the higher dimensional realms. Cynthia lives in Sedona, Arizona, with her husband, Pat, and Cavalier King Charles Spaniel, Kona.

Made in the USA
Las Vegas, NV
02 March 2024